NARCISSISM NAVIGATED

Harnessing AI for Personal Growth

DR. AMITA PURI, MS. SAUMYA JOGY
MS. ASTHA PURI, DR. BRAHMDEEP SINDHU
DR. SWATI SINDHU

New Delhi • London

BLUEROSE PUBLISHERS
India | U.K.

Copyright © Dr. Amita Puri, Ms. Saumya Jogy, Ms. Astha Puri,
Dr. Brahmdeep Sindhu, Dr. Swati Sindhu 2024

All rights reserved by author. No part of this publication may be reproduced, stored in a retrieval system or transmitted in any form or by any means, electronic, mechanical, photocopying, recording or otherwise, without the prior permission of the author. Although every precaution has been taken to verify the accuracy of the information contained herein, the publisher assume no responsibility for any errors or omissions. No liability is assumed for damages that may result from the use of information contained within.

BlueRose Publishers takes no responsibility for any damages, losses, or liabilities that may arise from the use or misuse of the information, products, or services provided in this publication.

For permissions requests or inquiries regarding this publication, please contact:

BLUEROSE PUBLISHERS
www.BlueRoseONE.com
info@bluerosepublishers.com
+91 8882 898 898
+4407342408967

ISBN: 978-93-6452-241-0

Cover design: Tahira
Typesetting: Tanya Raj Upadhyay

First Edition: August 2024

Dedication:

In loving memory of my late father, Dr. S.K. Verma, and my late mother, Smt. Kamlesh Verma.

Your wisdom and guidance continue to light my path, even in your absence. I miss you both dearly and cherish the love you gave me.

Your presence remains in my heart, inspiring me every day.

Forever grateful, forever loved.

As Narcissus had scorned her, so he had scorned the other nymphs of the rivers and mountains, so he had scorned the companies of young men. Then one of those who had been mocked, lifting hands to the skies, said 'So may he himself love, and so may he fail to command what he loves!' Rhamnusia, who is the goddess Nemesis, heard this just request.

There was an unclouded fountain, with silver-bright water, which neither shepherds nor goats grazing the hills, nor other flocks, touched, that no animal or bird disturbed not even a branch falling from a tree. Grass was around it, fed by the moisture nearby, and a grove of trees that prevented the sun from warming the place. Here, the boy, tired by the heat and his enthusiasm for the chase, lies down, drawn to it by its look and by the fountain. While he desires to quench his thirst, a different thirst is created. While he drinks he is seized by the vision of his reflected form. He loves a bodiless dream. He thinks that a body, which is only a shadow. He is astonished by himself, and hangs there motionless, with a fixed expression, like a statue carved from Parian marble.

Flat on the ground, he contemplates two stars, his eyes, and his hair, fit for Bacchus, fit for Apollo, his youthful cheeks and ivory neck, the beauty of his face, the rose-flush mingled in the whiteness of snow, admiring everything for which he is himself admired. Unknowingly he desires himself, and the one who praises is himself praised, and, while he courts, is courted, so that, equally, he inflames and burns. How often he gave his lips in vain to the deceptive pool, how often, trying to embrace the neck he could see, he plunged his arms into the water, but could not catch himself within them! What he has seen he does not understand, but what he sees he is on fire for, and the same error both seduces and deceives his eyes.

Fool, why try to catch a fleeting image, in vain? What you search for is nowhere: turning away, what you love is lost! What you perceive is the shadow of reflected form: nothing of you is in it. It comes and stays with you, and leaves with you, if you can leave!

Bk III:402-436 Narcissus sees himself and falls in love

The Mirror's Edge
In shadows deep, where echoes fade,
A heart once whole, now bruised and frayed.
Beside the mirror's gleaming face,
Lies a soul, lost in its trace.
A narcissist, with eyes so cold,
Reflections are their love untold.
Their gaze, a well of self-admire,
Leaves others yearning, hearts afire.
Promises like wisps of air,
Vanishing, leaving despair.
Words that cut with hidden blades,
Trust erodes, and joy degrades.
Emotions tangled, like vines that choke,
A spirit fights, but rarely spoke.
In the dance of praise and blame,
Lives a constant shifting shame.
Control disguised as tender care,

Freedom's flight becomes so rare.
Dreams confined within their grip,
Hope and sorrow start to slip.
Silent tears on pillow's edge,
Voices stifled, no one to pledge.
Each day a struggle, steps so light,
To avoid the tempest, avoid the fight.
Yet in this storm, a strength is found,
A will to rise from hardened ground.
To break the chains of mirrored lies,
And seek the sun in open skies.
For in the heart, where pain does dwell,
Resides a flame that can compel.
A journey far from shadow's claim,
To rediscover one's true name.
So, to those who live in mirrored land,
Take my heart, and take my hand.
Together we can find the way,
To brighter nights and dawn's new day.

Foreword

In today's digital age, the fusion of psychology and technology has unlocked unprecedented opportunities for personal growth and self-discovery. "Narcissism Navigated: Harnessing AI for Personal Growth" stands at the forefront of this intersection, offering a pioneering exploration into how artificial intelligence can be leveraged as a tool for navigating the complex terrain of narcissistic personality patterns.

In this insightful and groundbreaking book, the authors embark on a journey to demystify narcissism, shedding light on its intricacies and providing readers with a roadmap for transformative change. By harnessing the power of AI, they offer a fresh perspective on self-reflection, personal development, and emotional well-being.

Through a blend of research, practical insights, and real-life examples, "Narcissism Navigated" invites readers to embark on a journey of self-discovery like never before. From understanding the nuances of narcissistic traits to implementing AI-driven strategies for growth, this book serves as a beacon of hope for individuals seeking to transcend the limitations of their personality patterns.

As we navigate the complexities of modern life, this book serves as a timely reminder that technology, when wielded wisely, has the potential to catalyze profound personal transformation. Whether you're grappling with narcissistic tendencies yourself or seeking to support others on their journey, "Narcissism Navigated" offers invaluable guidance and inspiration.

In a world where self-awareness is the cornerstone of growth, this book paves the way for a new era of empowerment—one where AI becomes not just a tool, but a trusted ally in the pursuit of self-mastery and fulfillment. It is with great enthusiasm that I recommend this book to you, confident in its ability to illuminate the path toward a brighter, more compassionate future.

This book is the first of its kind in India and I am glad this valuable gift of the authors to our country with Indian case studies will help millions out there who are suffering in silence….for years.

But they need'nt.

The help is here, in their hands.

Dr.Anju Sharma

Principal

Vivekananda College of Education

Kathua, J&K

Preface

Living with a narcissistic family member is like co-starring in a reality show where you didn't audition but somehow got cast as the sidekick. Every family dinner turns into their personal TED Talk, complete with unnecessary PowerPoints about their latest minor accomplishments. They have a magical ability to turn any compliment you receive into a story about their own greatness: "You got a promotion? That's nice. It reminds me of the time I single-handedly saved the company from financial ruin." Holidays are particularly special, as they somehow transform "Happy Birthday, Grandma" into "Let's Celebrate Me Day." But hey, on the bright side, you never have to worry about who's taking the last piece of cake—they're too busy looking in the mirror to notice.

In this spirit, we welcome you to "Narcissism Navigated: Harnessing AI for Personal Growth." This book represents a culmination of years of research, introspection, and collaboration aimed at exploring how to empower the individuals with narcissistic patterns and also the family members who suffer in silence cursing their fate everyday while tiptoeing around life with uncertainties.

Our journey began with a simple question: How can we leverage the power of technology to better understand and manage narcissism? What emerged from this inquiry is a comprehensive exploration into the ways in which AI can serve as a catalyst for transformative change, offering new avenues for self-reflection, insight, and growth.

In these pages, we invite you to embark on a voyage of discovery—a journey that traverses the landscapes of narcissism with curiosity, compassion, and courage. Drawing upon the latest research in psychology, neuroscience, and technology, we illuminate the multifaceted nature of narcissistic traits, dispelling myths and misconceptions along the way.

But this book is more than just a theoretical exploration. It is a practical guide—a roadmap for navigating the complexities of narcissism and harnessing the potential of AI to facilitate personal transformation. From AI-driven self-assessment tools to innovative strategies for emotional regulation, each chapter is designed to empower you on your path to growth and self-discovery.

We recognize that the topic of narcissism is a deeply personal one, and we approach it with sensitivity and empathy. Whether you are grappling with narcissistic tendencies yourself or seeking to support others on their journey, our hope is that this book will serve as a beacon of light—a source of inspiration and guidance in times of uncertainty.

As you delve into the pages that follow, we encourage you to approach this exploration with an open mind and a willing heart. Embrace the challenges, celebrate the victories, and remember that growth is a journey, not a destination. Together, let us embark on this transformative odyssey—one that promises to illuminate the path toward greater self-awareness, authenticity, and connection.

The fact that this book is in your hands means you're either fascinated by the subject of narcissism or you've just stumbled into the world's most entertaining self-help guide. Whether you're grappling with a narcissistic family member or wondering if you might have a touch of the narcissism bug yourself, you're in the right place. This book is your survival kit for navigating the mystical, mind-boggling reality of living with or dealing with narcissists.

Packed with insights and tools, it's designed to help you handle those who can't walk past a mirror without saying, "Lookin' good!" with grace and a sense of humor. Plus, if you suspect you have some narcissistic traits, this book is your friendly guide to dialing it down a notch—or at least making it work for you in a less annoying way. Get ready to laugh, learn, and empower yourself and your loved ones to handle narcissistic antics with style and confidence.

This book is a friendly handshake just for you.

Your Author's team

Dr Amita Puri

Ms Saumya Jogy

Ms Astha Puri

Dr Brahmdeep Sindhu

Dr Swati Sindhu

Acknowledgment

We extend our deepest gratitude to our patients and clients, whose interactions have profoundly enriched our understanding of narcissism. Through these encounters, we not only honed our skills but also gained invaluable insights into the complexities of this syndrome. The wisdom and perspectives shared with us have been truly priceless, shaping our approach and deepening our empathy. Each interaction offered us a unique glimpse into the intricacies of human behavior, and for that, we are profoundly grateful.

Your courage to share your stories and experiences has been a beacon of learning and growth for us. It is through your openness and trust that we have been able to delve deeper into the nuances of narcissism, refining our techniques and expanding our knowledge. These interactions have not only informed our professional journey but have also touched us personally, reminding us of the profound impact of empathy and understanding in healing and growth.

To all of you who have been part of this journey, thank you. Your contributions have been invaluable, and your influence on our work is immeasurable. You have been our greatest teachers, and we are forever indebted to you for the priceless insights you have provided.

Benefits of This Book – In Your Hands

A Beacon Through the Shadows
In pages bound with wisdom's light,
A guide emerges from the night.
Navigating paths so fraught,
With lessons hard experience taught.
This book, a beacon shining bright,
Dispels the shadows, brings to sight,
The traits and traps of narcissist's game,
Reclaims our peace, restores our name.
With every chapter, clarity grows,
Unveiling truths that knowledge sows.
Empathy and insight blend,
To heal, to guide, to comprehend.
A mirror held up to the face,
Of those who seek to dominate space.
It teaches how to stand our ground,
In voices strong, no longer bound.
Boundaries firm, yet kindly set,
In this wisdom, our lives reset.
We learn to see, to act, to steer,
Through storms of self that once were near.
Empowered now, we walk with grace,
No longer lost in their embrace.
We find our voice, our strength, our way,
With tools to guide us every day.

In understanding, freedom's found,
Our spirits lift from troubled ground.
This book, a map, a friend, a light,
Guides us from darkness into bright.
To navigate with hearts unbowed,
We rise above, unchained, unclouded.
For in these words, we find the key,
To live, to love, authentically.

Benefits 1.0

Think of this book on navigating narcissism as your all-in-one toolkit for dealing with those larger-than-life personalities in a way that keeps you sane and smiling. First up, you'll boost your self-awareness – because knowing when you're about to lose it is half the battle. Then, you'll master effective coping strategies, turning every encounter with a narcissist into a chance to showcase your zen-like patience.

Empowerment to change? Oh, absolutely. You'll learn how to subtly shift the dynamics so you're no longer the sidekick in their one-person show. With enhanced emotion regulation, you'll laugh instead of cry when they pull their usual stunts. Finally, you'll build authentic connections, even with those who think authenticity means 200 filters on Instagram. By the end, you'll be navigating narcissism like a pro, with a smile on your face and maybe even a little sympathy for those mirror-loving souls.

Yes, this book is for those who notice narcissistic patterns in themselves and who wish to work and transform themselves to lead a healthier and more fulfilled life. Benefits are as follows:

1. **Increased Self-Awareness**: Readers will gain insights into their own behaviors and thought patterns, enabling them to recognize narcissistic tendencies [4].
2. **Effective Coping Strategies**: The book offers practical techniques and coping mechanisms to deal

with narcissistic traits, fostering healthier relationships and self-perception.

3. **Empowerment to Change**: By understanding the roots of narcissism and learning about self-improvement strategies, readers will feel empowered to initiate positive changes in their lives.

4. **Enhanced Emotional Regulation**: Through psychological insights and AI-driven tools, readers can develop better emotional regulation skills, leading to reduced stress and improved well-being.

5. **Building Authentic Connections**: The book guides readers in cultivating genuine connections with others by addressing underlying issues that contribute to narcissistic behavior patterns.

Benefits 2.0

This book on navigating narcissism is your ultimate guide to surviving and thriving amidst the chaos of self-obsessed antics. Here's what you'll gain:

1. **Recognition Skills:** You'll become a narcissism detective, spotting those telltale signs faster than they can say, "But enough about you, let's talk about me."

2. **Boundary Setting**: Learn to draw the line in the sand without getting sand kicked in your face. You'll become a boundary-setting ninja, ensuring your needs don't get trampled in their ego stampede.

3. **Emotional Resilience:** Develop a thick skin and a sharp wit. You'll bounce back from their drama like a rubber ball, with a quip at the ready and your sanity intact.

4. **Empowerment**: Gain the confidence to stand your ground and flip the script. You'll transform from supporting actor to director in the epic saga of your life.

5. **Personal Growth**: Emerge from the narcissistic whirlwind stronger and wiser, with more self-awareness and emotional intelligence than you ever thought possible.

Overall, a book on navigating narcissism can provide valuable insights, tools, and support for adolescents, young adults, and middle-aged individuals as they navigate the complexities of relationships and work towards improving their quality of life.

By the end of this book, you'll be handling narcissists with grace, humor, and the kind of personal growth that makes even the most self-centered person take notice.

Benefits 3.0

this book on understanding and navigating narcissism is like your secret weapon for dealing with those self-obsessed drama kings and queens in your life. Here's what you'll get:

1. ***Understanding Narcissism**:* You'll become a master of spotting narcissistic behavior, so you can finally understand why your cousin thinks they're the star of every family gathering.

2. ***Validation Techniques:*** Learn the art of validating a narcissist just enough to keep them happy while keeping your own sanity intact. It's like handing them a gold star without selling your soul.

3. ***Communication Strategies**:* Discover how to talk to a narcissist without wanting to pull your hair out. You'll master the skill of navigating conversations where "me, myself, and I" isn't the only topic.

4. ***Setting Boundaries:*** Become an expert at drawing lines in the sand that even the most self-absorbed person can't cross. You'll protect your space and peace of mind like a pro.

5. ***Support and Coping Strategies**:* Find out how to build a support system and develop coping mechanisms that make dealing with narcissistic antics feel like a breeze.

6. ***Special Tips for Women**:* Empower yourself with strategies tailored for women, helping you handle narcissistic partners, friends, or family members without losing your cool or your sense of humor.

For those dealing with narcissistic family and friends, this book is a lifesaver. You'll gain the tools to navigate their inflated egos, set firm boundaries, and keep your own sense of self intact. Plus, you'll be armed with enough wit and wisdom to turn every narcissistic encounter into a comedy rather than a tragedy.

Benefit 4.0

Benefits of "Navigating Narcissism" for the Average Joe

So, you've never tangoed with a narcissist, huh? Lucky you! But wait, before you dismiss the book Navigating Narcissism as just a survival guide for the drama-prone, let's dive into how it can help even the most drama-free Joe:

1. **Recognition and Awareness:**

Picture this: you're at a party, someone's droning on about their third yacht (yawn), and suddenly it hits you – you're in the presence of a narcissist! Navigating Narcissism can turn you into a narcissist-detecting ninja. You'll be spotting them like a pro, and let's face it, that's a party trick right up there with pulling quarters from behind ears.

2. **Self-Protection:**

Now that you've identified the narcissist, this book is your shield. Think of it like an invisibility cloak for your ego. You'll dodge their manipulative mind games with the finesse of a matador avoiding a bull. Ole!

3. **Conflict Resolution:**

Imagine being able to defuse arguments with the grace of a Jedi mind-tricking an overly persistent stormtrooper. Instead of falling into their trap, you'll navigate conflicts so smoothly, you could probably get a job at the UN.

4. **Empathy and Compassion:**

Surprisingly, this book might even make you feel a bit sorry for narcissists. Yes, they're annoying, but they're also kinda pitiable, like that one guy who always talks about his fantasy football league. You'll learn to give them the emotional equivalent of a pat on the head and a "there, there."

5. **Community Support**:

Ever noticed how every social group seems to have at least one person who dominates the conversation? With your new skills, you'll become the hero of your group, offering sage advice and subtle eye-rolls that say, "We've got this." Plus, you'll get invited to all the cool gatherings for being the Narcissist Whisperer.

6. Personal Growth:

Finally, Navigating Narcissism is like a gym membership for your mind. You'll build up your emotional resilience, flex those self-care muscles, and maybe even tone down your own (very minor, totally charming) narcissistic tendencies. Think of it as mental CrossFit – without the annoying Facebook check-ins.

So, whether you're brushing shoulders with CEOs or just trying to get through family dinners without losing your cool, this book can be your secret weapon. Who knew that avoiding narcissists could make you the most balanced, empathetic, and conflict-savvy guy on the block? Happy navigating!

Disclaimer:

This book is intended solely for educational and informational purposes. It is not intended for diagnosing or treating any mental health condition. The content within this book is not a substitute for professional advice or therapy.

This book is not intended to be used as a tool for manipulation or exploitation or defamation of individuals with narcissistic traits or that of any other personality disorders. It is not intended to provide any sort of strategies to exploit or harm anyone.

This book is not suitable for audience who are seeking quick fixes or shortcuts to address complex psychological issues. It is also not suitable for those who are unwilling to engage on genuine self-reflection and personal growth.

This book is not intended to create judgement or stigma against individuals with narcissistic traits. Rather, it aims at fostering understanding and embracing strategies for growth and well-being.

Readers with severe mental health concerns, including but not limited to Narcissistic Personality Disorder, are advised to seek professional help from a qualified mental health professional. This book does not replace the need for personalized therapy and treatment.

Legal disclaimer: The authors disclaim any liability, loss or risk incurred as a consequence , directly or indirectly of the use of this book in a manner that was not in line with the basic spirit and intention behind this book.

Table of Contents

Dedication: .... *iii*

Foreword .... *viii*

Preface .... *x*

Acknowledgment .... *xiii*

Benefits of This Book – In Your Hands .... *xv*

Benefits 1.0 .... *xvii*

Benefits 2.0 .... *xix*

Benefits 3.0 .... *xxi*

Benefit 4.0 .... *xxiii*

Disclaimer: .... *xxv*

Chapter 1: Understanding Narcissism 1
   Understanding Narcissism: 1
   Case Study: Sunita and Arun: 3
   Origins of Narcissism 7
   Characteristics of Narcissism 8
   Understanding Narcissism: Key Differences Between Individuals with NPD Traits and Others 11
   Symptoms of NPD as seen across different age groups: 15
   Helping Family Members Adapt 17
   Implications for Personal Growth and Wellbeing 19

Chapter 2: The Intersection of Psychology and Technology 21
   The Rise of Artificial Intelligence (AI) 21
   AI in Mental Health Care 22

Why have we proposed integrating AI into our approach to managing narcissism?................23

Benefits of AI in Mental Health for Individuals with NPD..................25

Benefits of AI To Family Members............................29

Looking Ahead..32

Chapter 3: Self-Awareness..34

Why is Gaining Insight into Narcissistic Personality Patterns and Fostering Self-Awareness Important?........34

Empirically Supported Therapies for NPD and the Role of Self-Discovery and Self-Awareness.................37

Willingness to Change and Narcissistic Personality Disorder (NPD)..............................39

The Power of Self-Reflection- with AI self assessment tools..40

AI-Driven Self-Assessment Tools- Assess yourself......40

AI Assisted Insights Leading To Personal Growth For Individuals With NPD..41

AI-Assisted Insights Leading To Professional Growth For Individuals With NPD 43

Empowering Personal Growth.....................................44

How can friends and family navigate being around Patient of NPD who lacks self-awareness?....................45

How AI and other technological tools can can help friends and family of NPD patients who lack self-awareness. and how these tools can make their lives better..46

Embracing AI for Self-Awareness and NPD Management: A Call to Innovate..................................47

Simple and Do-able: Steps for NPD patients to Navigate and improve self-awareness:.........................49

Case study: Narcissistic Tendencies- Jai's Story of Realization and Recovery 51

Chapter 4: From Awareness to Action: Implementing AI Strategies for Behavioural Change 56

What does it mean to move from self awareness to real change? 57

Need for Exploring Strategies to Address Narcissistic Personality Patterns and Facilitate Meaningful Personal Growth 58

Empathy and NPD 59

Therapy and Behavioural Change in NPD patients 61

Identifying Maladaptive Patterns 62

Setting Goals for Change 66

Implementing Behavior Change Strategies 70

Monitoring Progress and Adjusting Strategies 75

Obstacles In Implementing AI Strategies For Personal Growth In Individuals With Npd 83

Chapter 5: Overcoming Narcissistic Challenges: AI-Driven Techniques for Emotional Regulation 89

Understanding Emotions 90

Emotional Regulation 91

Emotional Dysregulation and Narcissistic Personality Disorder (NPD) 93

Empathy and Narcissistic Personality Disorder (NPD) . 97

Emotional regulation for those suffering from NPD 99
  The Role of Friends and Family in Supporting Emotional Regulation for Individuals with NPD 101

AI-Driven Emotion Recognition – Responsible AI 103

Development of AI-Based Tools for Emotional Regulation: 103

Functionalities of AI-Based Tools for Emotional Regulation: 104

Obstacles In Implementing Overcoming Narcissistic Challenges with AI For Regulating Emotions 105

Cultivating Mindfulness and Self-Compassion 106

Building Interpersonal Skills 107

Embracing AI for Emotional Regulation and NPD Management: A Call to Innovate 108

Ethical Considerations in AI-Based Tools for Emotional Regulation: 110

Future Directions and Challenges: 111

Case study- The Journey of Mrs. Reema: A Tale of Redemption 112

Chapter 6: Nurturing Empathy and Connection: AI's Role in Enhancing Interpersonal Relationships 116

Characteristics of NPD and Relationship Impact 117

Red Flags and Early Warning Signs of Narcissistic Personality Disorder (NPD) in Relationships 118

Prioritizing your wellbeing when you notice the red flags 120

Therapeutic Approaches in Interpersonal relationship management of NPD patients 121

Navigating Relationships with NPD Individuals 126

Setting Boundaries and Developing Support Systems 126

Effective Communication and Conflict Resolution Strategies 128

Practical Examples and Scenarios 130

AI-Driven Mental Health Apps and Virtual Support Groups 132

    Harnessing AI for Interpersonal Relationship Enhancement and NPD Management: A Call to Innovate 135

    Case Study: Love, Control, and Resilience: Reena's Journey to Self-Empowerment 138

Chapter 7: Nurturing Empathy and Connection: AI's Role in Enhancing Interpersonal Relationships- 142

    Are NPD Patients Monsters? Shifting Perspectives: From Demonization to Understanding 142

    Can people with NPD change? 146

    Do Patients with NPD Feel Guilt and Regret? 148

    How can you empathise with someone who causes you pain? 149

    Differentiating empathy from forgiveness 152

    Understanding Guilt and Self-Blame in Non-NPD Individuals with NPD Loved Ones 154

    Ensuring the Psychological Well-being of Children with Narcissistic Parents 157

    Navigating relationship with an NPD patient with poor prognosis 160

    AI as a Compassionate Resource: Supporting NPD Individuals and Their Loved Ones 163

    Building Empathy in NPD Individuals with AI 164

    Supporting Families and Loved Ones with AI 165

    Improving Interpersonal Relationships with AI 166

    Case study-The Entrepreneur's Struggle: Raj's Journey with NPD and the Role of AI 167

Chapter 8: Embracing Change: AI as a Catalyst for Lasting Transformation 171

    AI-Driven Habit Formation and Change 171

    Personalized Learning and Growth Pathways 172

- Enhancing Self-Awareness Through Feedback Loops 172
- Overcoming Resistance Through AI Engagement 173
- Long-Term Progress Monitoring 173
- Virtual Therapeutic Environments 173
- Sustaining Transformation through Community and Support 174
- Limitations Of Behaviour Modification With AI For Lasting Behaviour Change 174

Chapter 9: The Future of AI and Personal Development: Ethical Considerations and Beyond 176

- Ethical Use of AI in Personal Development 177
- Legal And Regulatory Challenges In AI-Driven Personal Development 177
- Bias and Fairness 178
- The Role of Human Oversight 179
- Future Directions in AI and Narcissistic Personality Development 179
- Societal Implications and the Path Forward 179
- Challenges in the Future of AI in the management of NPD 180

Chapter 10: Navigating the Journey Ahead: Empowering Individuals and Communities 182

- Empowering Individuals for Sustainable Change 183
- Strengthening Community Bonds 183
- The Role of AI in Education and Awareness 183
- Ethical and Inclusive Development of AI Tools 184
- Looking Forward: A Collaborative Vision for the Future 184
  - Case Study: Mrs. Gupta - A Female Narcissist 185

Chapter 11: Beyond the Book: Implementing Change in the Real World 187
    Practical Implementation of AI Tools 187
    Creating Accessible and Inclusive AI Solutions 188
    Building Partnerships for Wider Impact 188
    Fostering a Culture of Continuous Learning and Adaptation 189
    Advocating for Ethical Standards and Regulation 189
    Challenges to implementing changes in the real world of repairing from narcissistic abuse 189
    Conclusion 191

Chapter 12: A Call to Action: Mobilizing a Community for Change 192
    Empowering Individuals with Knowledge and Tools . 192
    Encouraging Professional Engagement and Development 193
    Fostering Ethical AI Development 193
    Building Community Support Systems 194
    Advocating for Policy and Societal Change 194
    Conclusion: A Collective Journey Forward 194

Chapter 13: Envisioning the Future: AI and the Evolution of Personal Development 196
    The Next Generation of AI Tools 196
    AI as a Catalyst for Deeper Self-Understanding 197
    Bridging the Gap Between AI and Human Connection 197
    The Role of AI in Creating a More Empathetic Society 198
    Ethical Considerations and Human Agency 198
    A Collaborative Future 198

In Conclusion 199
Management through Collaborative Approach 199
Conclusion 201
How AI can help in Managing Narcissistic
Personality Patterns 202
AI and Subconscious Energy Healing for
Narcissistic Personality Patterns 209
Optimism and hope for victims of abuse from
Narsisistic Individuals 215
In Conclusion: Empowerment Through
Understanding and Collaboration 217
Glossary 218

Chapter 1:
Understanding Narcissism

We've all encountered people who exhibit narcissistic traits in our daily lives. The term "narcissist" is commonly used to describe individuals who appear self-absorbed or overly self-important. The concept of narcissism originates from Greek mythology, where Narcissus, a handsome young man, falls in love with his own reflection. This term has evolved to describe a complex and multifaceted personality trait that presents itself in various ways across different individuals.

In this chapter, we will explore the essence of narcissism—its roots, defining characteristics, and its implications for personal development and well-being.

Understanding Narcissism:

Understanding narcissism is like trying to befriend a peacock: you're dazzled by the feathers until you realize it's all about them. A narcissist is that person who, when asked to pass the salt, gives you their life story instead because, well, you asked for it, didn't you?

In personal relationships, dating a narcissist can feel like you're the supporting actor in a one-person show. Imagine a romantic dinner where your partner gazes deeply into your eyes... only to catch their own reflection in your glasses. Yes, it's always their day, every day. You might find yourself listening to endless monologues about their latest achievement, while your own tales get cut short faster than a sneeze.

Professionally, working with a narcissist is akin to climbing a corporate ladder that's missing rungs—thanks to someone who took them to build their own pedestal. Team projects quickly turn into solo acts, where your ideas get applauded only if someone else can take credit for them. Narcissists excel in meetings where the agenda is "Look at me!", and you're left wondering if the mirror in the bathroom gets more daily affirmations than you do.

In both spheres, relationships with narcissists are a high-wire act of balancing their ego with your sanity. It's a tightrope that offers no safety net, just a reminder that, in their world, everything revolves around them. And if you ever forget that, don't worry—they'll remind you. Repeatedly.

The issue and understanding of narcissistic personality patterns have gained significant public attention, especially with the high-profile case of Johnny Depp and Amber Heard. This courtroom drama played out like a blockbuster, complete with plot twists, shocking revelations, and enough emotional turbulence to rival any Hollywood script.

Narcissism, in this context, can be illustrated by examining the tumultuous dynamics between Depp and Heard. Their relationship, which once seemed like a fairy tale, spiraled into a nightmare filled with allegations of abuse, manipulation, and toxic behavior. For those observing from the outside, it became a case study in how narcissistic traits can manifest and wreak havoc in personal relationships.

Remember Johnny Depp and Amber Heard's (in)famous case?

The case revealed patterns often associated with narcissistic personalities, such as gaslighting, where one partner manipulates the other into doubting their own reality. Both parties accused each other of such behavior, showcasing how destructive and confusing narcissistic dynamics can be. The publicized nature of their conflict offered a stark look at how narcissistic traits, like the need for control and the insatiable craving for attention, can lead to a toxic cycle of blame and victimization.

In the professional realm, the Depp-Heard saga also highlights how narcissistic tendencies can impact careers. Both actors faced significant reputational damage, lost opportunities, and intense public scrutiny. It became clear that when narcissistic patterns emerge in professional settings, the fallout can be just as devastating as in personal relationships. Careers can be derailed, and the workplace environment can become a battleground of egos, accusations, and power plays.

Lets look at this case study to understand and navigate narcissism better.

Case Study: Sunita and Arun:

Background:

Sunita and Arun have been married for eight years, a time filled with ups, downs, and a lot of "look at me" moments. Recently, Arun filed for divorce, citing irreconcilable differences. The court has suggested mediation, and here they are, sitting on opposite ends of the couch in your office, ready for a last-ditch attempt at reconciliation.

Sunita's Personality Patterns:

Sunita's behavior exhibits several classic symptoms of Narcissistic Personality Disorder (NPD):

1. **Grandiosity:** Sunita often talks about her achievements, real or imagined, as if she's narrating a best-seller. Whether it's her latest work project or a minor cooking success, everything is a triumph of epic proportions.

2. **Need for Admiration**: Sunita requires constant validation. Arun's attempts to discuss his own successes or concerns are usually met with swift redirection back to her. Compliments must flow in one direction only.

3. **Lack of Empathy:** When Arun discusses his feelings, Sunita's responses range from indifference to outright dismissal. Arun once compared his feelings to talking to a wall—except the wall at least doesn't interrupt.

4. **Sense of Entitlement**: Sunita expects special treatment. Arun recounts countless dinners where Sunita expected the waiter to not just serve food but to applaud her menu choices.

5. **Interpersonal Exploitative Behaviors:** Sunita often takes advantage of Arun's kindness. She once made Arun stay up all night helping her prepare a presentation for work, only to take all the credit without so much as a thank you.

Mediation Session Highlights:

During the session, it becomes clear that Sunita's behavior fits the NPD profile. Here's a snapshot of their interaction:

Arun: "I feel overwhelmed with our financial planning. We never seem to discuss things."

Sunita: "Oh please, you're just not good with money. Remember how I single-handedly negotiated our mortgage? I'm practically a financial genius!"

Arun: "I'm really hurt that you never appreciate my efforts with the kids."

Sunita: "You're hurt? Imagine how I feel when you don't notice how perfectly I manage the house despite my busy schedule. I'm the real hero here."

Technical Evaluation:

Using standardized tools such as the DSM-5 criteria for NPD, Sunita's behavior can be objectively assessed. She meets at least five of the nine criteria necessary for an NPD diagnosis, confirming the disorder.

Interplay with Other Disorders:

Sunita's case also shows hints of Histrionic Personality Disorder (HPD), characterized by attention-seeking behaviors and excessive emotionality. This blend of narcissistic and histrionic traits makes her interactions a dramatic spectacle, as she often oscillates between demanding admiration and creating emotional scenes to be the center of attention.

Recommendations:

1. For Sunita

- Therapy: Engage in long-term psychotherapy focused on developing empathy and improving interpersonal skills.

- Mindfulness: Practice mindfulness techniques to help her stay present and understand others' perspectives.

2. For Arun:

- Boundaries: Establish clear boundaries to protect his own emotional well-being.

- Support: Seek individual counseling to process his experiences and develop coping strategies.

3. For Family and Friends:

- Awareness: Be aware of signs of NPD and HPD, such as excessive need for admiration and dramatic behaviors.

- Support: Offer support without enabling. Encourage professional help when necessary.

- Self-Care: Take care of their own mental health and set boundaries to avoid being overwhelmed by the narcissist's needs.

Important Takeaway:

Think of Sunita as the star of a one-woman show where every seat is a front-row ticket to her life's drama. The best way to survive her performance? Enjoy the spectacle from a distance, throw popcorn when appropriate, and always have a good exit strategy. And remember, in Sunita's theater, applause isn't just appreciated—it's mandatory.

Origins of Narcissism

We began thi book with a short excerpt from the poem Metamorphasis by the roman poet Ovid. The term 'narcissism' originated from here. As the myth goes, Narcissus was a beautiful young man who spurned the affections of others, including the nymph Echo. He became infatuated with his own reflection in a pool of water. He was unable to tear himself away from his spot at the pool side and eventually he wasted away and perished after being consumed by love for his own reflection.

Havelock Ellis linked this myth to the condition of "auto-eroticism" (i.e. self as own sexual object) seen in one of his patients and was the first psychologist to clinically use the term "Narcissus-like"

Freud similarly first used the terms "ego-libido" (self-love) and "narcissistic libido" interchangeably in his Three Essays on the Theory of Sexuality. Freud, introduced the term to describe an excessive preoccupation with oneself and one's own needs. Ellis' and Freud's psychoanalytic narcissism both included an immature, exclusively self-gratifying sexuality that is not necessarily a part of its clinical definition today.

Ernest Jones was the first to construe narcissism as a character trait which he called the "God-complex." He described people with the God-complex as aloof, inaccessible, self-admiring, self-important, overconfident, auto-erotic, and exhibitionistic, with fantasies of omnipotence and omniscience. He also observed that these people had a high need for uniqueness ("…nothing offends such a man as the suggestion that he resembles someone else…" p. 252) and praise from others. This description is remarkably close to the current conception of At nearly the same time Freud.

Over time, scholars and researchers have expanded upon these initial theories, offering new insights into the nature and development of narcissistic personality patterns.

Narcissism can manifest in different ways, ranging from grandiosity and arrogance to insecurity and hypersensitivity.

Characteristics of Narcissism

Central to the concept of narcissism are certain key characteristics that distinguish it from other personality traits. These include:

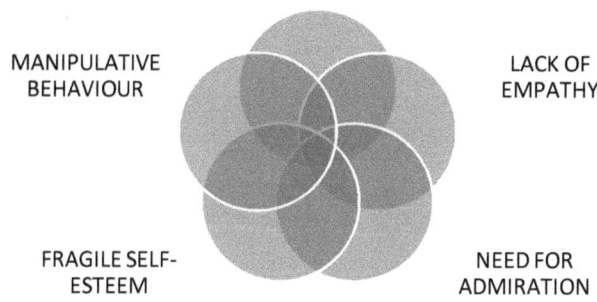

1. Grandiosity: A sense of superiority and entitlement, often accompanied by fantasies of success, power, and admiration.

2. Lack of Empathy: Difficulty understanding and empathizing with the emotions and experiences of others.

3. Need for Admiration: A constant craving for attention, admiration, and validation from others.

4. Fragile Self-Esteem: Despite outward displays of confidence, narcissistic individuals often harbor deep-seated insecurities and vulnerabilities.

5. Manipulative Behavior: A tendency to exploit and manipulate others to achieve one's own goals and desires.

While some individuals exhibit **overt narcissistic** traits, such as a sense of entitlement and a lack of empathy, others may **display covert narcissism**, characterized by self-pity and a constant need for validation.

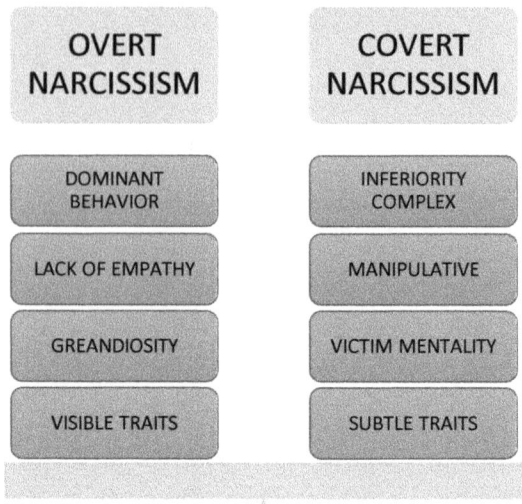

There are two types of narcissism

1. **Overt Narcissism**:

    - **Visible Traits**: Overt narcissists display their narcissistic traits openly and prominently.

    - **Grandiosity**: They often exhibit grandiose behaviors, seek attention, and exaggerate their achievements.

    - **Lack of Empathy**: They show a lack of empathy towards others and may exploit them for personal gain.

    - **Dominant Behavior**: Overt narcissists tend to dominate social interactions and seek admiration from others.

- **Externalizing Blame**: They may externalize blame and refuse to take responsibility for their actions.

2. **Covert Narcissism**:
    - **Subtle Traits**: Covert narcissists hide their narcissistic traits behind a facade of humility or shyness.
    - **Victim Mentality**: They often portray themselves as victims, seeking sympathy and validation from others.
    - **Manipulative**: Covert narcissists manipulate others through passive-aggressive behaviors and emotional manipulation.
    - **Inferiority Complex**: Despite their outward humility, they harbor feelings of superiority and entitlement.
    - **Internalizing Blame**: They may internalize blame and play the role of the misunderstood or mistreated individual

Thus, overt narcissists openly display narcissistic traits, seek attention, lack empathy, and may exploit others. Covert narcissists, on the other hand may hide their traits behind humility, play victim, manipulate others, and feel superior internally.

Understanding Narcissism: Key Differences Between Individuals with NPD Traits and Others

1. **Empathy**: Those with Narcissistic Personality Disorder (NPD) often struggle with empathy, unlike

individuals without the disorder who can typically empathize with others.

2. **Self-Importance**: People with NPD tend to inflate their importance, achievements, and talents, often exaggerating them. This trait is less common in the general population.

3. **Relationships**: Individuals with NPD may have turbulent and shallow relationships due to their need for excessive admiration and lack of empathy, disregarding others' feelings and needs. Those without NPD generally seek more balanced and reciprocal relationships.

4. **Sensitivity to Criticism**: Those with NPD can be highly sensitive to criticism or perceived slights, often reacting with anger or significant upset. This sensitivity is not as pronounced in individuals without the disorder.

5. **Self-Perception**: While everyone may display moments of selfishness or vanity, individuals with NPD often live in a state of grandiosity and fantasy about their success, beauty, brilliance, etc., which can disconnect them from reality.

To understand the above better lets imagine you're at a party. The person with Narcissistic Personality Disorder (NPD) is easy to spot: they're the one standing under a spotlight, wearing a sash that reads "Most Amazing Person Ever," and talking non-stop about their latest and greatest achievements—even if it's just about how they microwaved popcorn to perfection.

Now, compare this to the regular partygoer without NPD. They're mingling, genuinely asking others how they've been, and maybe sharing a funny story about their dog getting stuck in the laundry basket. They enjoy being part of the conversation, not the whole show.

Here's a humorous breakdown which looks comical to others but the NPD individual sees nothing extraordinary about it.

- **Attention**

- NPD: "Let's talk about me. Enough about you, let's hear what you think about me."

- Non-NPD: "Tell me about your vacation! That sounds exciting."

- **Achievements**:

- NPD: "I once saved a company from bankruptcy, invented a new type of sandwich, and won a staring contest with a cat—all before lunch."

- Non-NPD: "I had a pretty productive week. Got some work done, enjoyed a good book."

- **Empathy**:

- NPD: "You're sad? Ugh, that's inconvenient for me. Can we focus on my latest success instead?"

- Non-NPD: "I'm sorry to hear that. Do you want to talk about it?"

- **Criticism:**

- NPD: "Criticize me? How dare you! I am flawless!"

- Non-NPD: "Thanks for the feedback. I'll work on that."

-Conversations:

- **NPD:** A monologue about their greatness, sprinkled with condescension.

- **Non-NPD**: A dialogue where everyone gets to share and feel heard.

In essence, while everyone enjoys a little recognition now and then, the person with NPD takes it to an Olympic level. They're not just part of the party—they are the party, and everyone else is there to serve as their adoring audience. Non-NPD folks, on the other hand, are there to share the fun, listen, and enjoy the company.

But, remember, exhibiting some traits associated with NPD does not necessarily mean someone has the disorder. Diagnosis requires a comprehensive evaluation by mental health professionals.

Diagnosing Narcissistic Personality Disorder (NPD)

Understanding the common characteristics of narcissism may lead to recognition of these traits in oneself or others. However, it's crucial to distinguish between exhibiting narcissistic traits and having Narcissistic Personality Disorder (NPD).

NPD is a mental health condition characterized by consistent display of traits like grandiosity or lack of empathy. It falls under Cluster B personality disorders, known for dramatic, emotional, and erratic behaviors. Individuals with NPD often exhibit an extreme form of self-centeredness that significantly impacts their daily and interpersonal interactions.

However, not everyone displaying narcissistic traits meets the diagnostic criteria for NPD. Diagnosis requires thorough assessment by a clinician. For example, someone may demonstrate self-centered tendencies but not qualify for an NPD diagnosis upon assessment. They may possess narcissistic character traits without meeting the full criteria for the disorder.

It's essential to approach the diagnosis of NPD with caution and rely on professional evaluation to differentiate between narcissistic traits and the disorder itself. Understanding this difference is crucial for accurate diagnosis and appropriate intervention.

Symptoms of NPD as seen across different age groups:

1. Grandiose sense of self-importance:

- Adolescent: Constantly boasting about their achievements on social media to gain attention and validation from peers.

- Young adulthood: Believing they are destined for greatness and disregarding others' opinions or advice because they consider themselves superior.

- Middle age: Insisting on always being the center of attention in social gatherings and monopolizing conversations with stories about their accomplishments.

- Old age: Continuously reminiscing about their past achievements and exaggerating their importance in historical events during conversations with family members.

2. Need for excessive admiration:

- Adolescent: Frequently seeking validation from friends and classmates for their appearance, talents, or achievements.

- Young adulthood: Expecting constant praise and admiration from coworkers or romantic partners, becoming upset or angry if they don't receive it.

- Middle age: Requiring admiration from subordinates in the workplace and becoming irritable if their authority is questioned.

- Old age: Demanding admiration from adult children and grandchildren, feeling offended if they are not acknowledged as the family's patriarch or matriarch.

3. Lack of empathy for others:

- Adolescent: Bullying or belittling peers without considering the emotional impact of their actions.

- Young adulthood: Manipulating others to achieve their goals without regard for their feelings or well-being.

- Middle age: Exploiting colleagues or employees for personal gain without considering the consequences for their livelihoods or emotions.

- Old age: Dismissing the needs or concerns of caregivers or nursing home staff, expecting them to cater to their every whim without considering their own workload or emotional state.

4. Sense of entitlement:

- Adolescent: Expecting special treatment or privileges from parents, teachers, or authority figures without earning them.

- Young adulthood: Feeling entitled to success, wealth, or admiration without putting in the necessary effort or hard work.

- Middle age: Believing they deserve preferential treatment in professional settings, such as promotions or raises, based solely on their perceived superiority.

- Old age: Demanding preferential treatment from healthcare providers or service personnel due to their age or social status, disregarding the needs of others in similar situations.

These examples illustrate how narcissistic traits can manifest across different stages of life, impacting relationships and social interactions in various ways.

Helping Family Members Adapt

Understanding narcissistic personality disorder (NPD) can significantly help family members of individuals with the disorder in several key ways, particularly in improving their own self-worth and navigating the challenging dynamics that can arise. Here are a few insights into how this understanding can be beneficial:

1. **Recognizing the Source of Issues**

- Depersonalizing Negative Behaviors: Understanding that certain behaviors stem from the disorder rather than personal failings can help family members not take hurtful actions or words as personally. This recognition can protect their self-worth by attributing difficulties to the condition, not to something being "wrong" with them.

2. **Setting Healthy Boundaries**

- Protecting Emotional Well-being: By comprehending the nature of NPD, family members can learn to set and enforce healthy boundaries to protect their emotional well-being. Boundaries can help manage expectations and interactions, preventing family members from being overly drained or feeling responsible for the narcissistic individual's emotional state.

3. Seeking Support and Resources

- Building a Support Network: Understanding the challenges of living with someone with NPD can encourage family members to seek support, whether through therapy, support groups, or education on the disorder. This network can reinforce their self-worth by validating their experiences and providing coping strategies.

4. Adjusting Communication Strategies

- Effective Communication: Gaining insights into how people with NPD perceive criticism, praise, and attention can guide family members in adjusting their communication strategies to reduce conflict and misunderstanding, helping to maintain a more peaceful home environment.

5. Cultivating Personal Growth

- Focus on Personal Development: Understanding the disorder can motivate family members to focus on their own personal growth and self-care, recognizing the importance of not being entirely consumed by the narcissistic individual's needs and behaviors.

6. Realistic Expectations

- Managing Expectations: By acknowledging the limitations of the disorder, family members can set more realistic expectations for the relationship, reducing disappointment and frustration. This adjustment can help maintain their self-worth by not basing it on the approval or recognition from the person with NPD.

7. **Empowering Choices**

- Making Informed Decisions: With a deeper understanding of NPD, family members can make informed decisions about their level of engagement or the need for professional intervention, which can be empowering and affirm their self-worth.

Understanding narcissistic personality disorder doesn't make the challenges disappear, but it equips family members with tools and perspectives that are crucial for navigating these relationships while preserving and even improving their sense of self-worth. It encourages an approach that balances empathy for the individual with NPD with a firm commitment to self-care and emotional health.

Implications for Personal Growth and Wellbeing

While narcissism is often portrayed in a negative light, it is important to recognize that it exists on a spectrum, and not all narcissistic traits are inherently harmful. In fact, some degree of narcissism can be adaptive, providing individuals with the confidence and drive to pursue their goals and aspirations.

However, when narcissistic tendencies become excessive or maladaptive, they can impede personal growth and undermine interpersonal relationships. It is essential, therefore, to cultivate self-awareness and mindfulness to navigate the complexities of narcissism and harness its potential for positive change.

In the chapters that follow, we will explore how artificial intelligence can serve as a valuable tool for understanding and managing narcissistic personality patterns. By leveraging the power of technology, we can gain new insights into our own behavior, develop healthier coping mechanisms, and embark on a journey of self-discovery and personal growth.

Let us embark on this exploration with an open mind and a willingness to learn, for it is through understanding and compassion that we can truly transcend the limitations of narcissism and embrace the fullness of our humanity.

Chapter 2:
The Intersection of Psychology and Technology

In this chapter, we delve into the convergence of psychology and technology, exploring how artificial intelligence (AI) has emerged as a powerful tool for enhancing self-awareness, facilitating personal growth, and transforming the landscape of mental health care. As we navigate the complexities of narcissism, we recognize the unique opportunities that AI presents for gaining insight into our own behavior and fostering positive change.

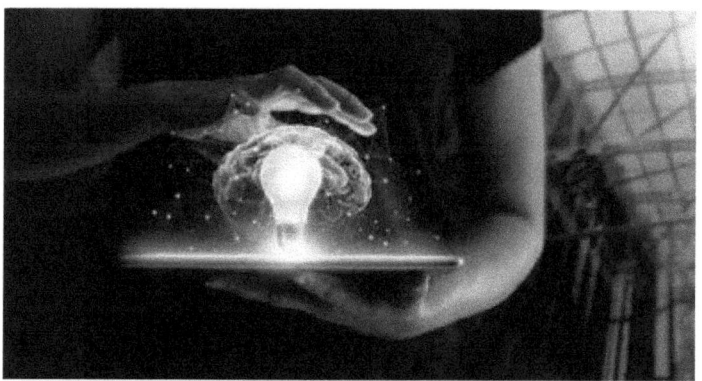

The Rise of Artificial Intelligence (AI)

Once a staple of science fiction, artificial intelligence has swiftly integrated into our everyday lives. From virtual assistants like Siri to sophisticated machine learning algorithms, AI technologies have reshaped how we access information, communicate, and interact with the world.

At its essence, AI consists of a diverse set of technologies and methodologies designed to emulate human cognitive functions such as learning, reasoning, and problem-solving. Machine learning, a subset of AI, involves creating algorithms capable of analyzing data, recognizing patterns, and making predictions without explicit instructions.

In this book, we refer to AI as any technology harnessing artificial intelligence algorithms to enhance therapeutic outcomes. This broad definition includes various AI applications, gadgets, and tools dedicated to offering therapeutic value for addressing narcissistic traits. Specifically, AI enables personalized interventions, real-time feedback, and customized support for individuals dealing with narcissism.

Through this convergence of AI and psychology, we embark on a journey to leverage cutting-edge technology for deeper self-understanding and meaningful personal development.

AI in Mental Health Care

In recent years, AI has emerged as a game-changer in mental health care, revolutionizing how we assess, diagnose, and treat various conditions. Harnessing the power of data analytics, natural language processing, and predictive modeling, AI opens up thrilling new possibilities for mental wellness.

When it comes to treatment and management of NPD, AI has endless potential . Imagine AI-driven self-assessment tools that act like personal mirrors, reflecting your behavior and offering deep insights. Picture virtual coaching platforms that feel like having a personal growth guru at your fingertips. These AI innovations can help individuals recognize harmful patterns, cultivate self-awareness, and craft personalized strategies for meaningful change.

With AI, the journey to better mental health becomes not just possible but also exciting and engaging, turning self-improvement into an adventure of discovery and growth.

Why have we proposed integrating AI into our approach to managing narcissism?

There are several compelling reasons:

1. **Ease of Use**: AI tools like ChatGPT have become indispensable in daily tasks, whether it's helping with homework, composing a birthday greeting, or drafting an email. This widespread adoption is largely due to the convenience and efficiency these tools offer. By leveraging AI for managing narcissism, we aim to bring the same level of ease and seamlessness to the treatment and management of Narcissistic Personality Disorder (NPD). AI can streamline processes, making it simpler for patients and therapists to interact and engage in treatment activities.

2. **Increased Autonomy**: AI acts as a personal assistant, enabling individuals to perform tasks more effectively and independently. For NPD patients, AI can provide tools and resources that empower them to take greater control over their treatment. This increased autonomy can be crucial in helping them feel more self-sufficient and capable of managing their condition.

3. **Constant Availability**: NPD is a chronic condition that requires ongoing attention and support. However, therapists and family members may not always be available to provide the necessary support. AI-driven technologies can fill this gap by offering continuous assistance and monitoring. This ensures that patients have access to support whenever they need it, enhancing the overall effectiveness of the treatment.

Also, here's a light-hearted take on using AI to manage narcissism or narcissistic personality disorder:

Introducing the revolutionary AI system, "EgoTamer 3000," designed specifically for handling the most challenging narcissistic personalities! Here's how it works:

1. **Mirror Mode**: EgoTamer 3000 comes with a virtual mirror that offers constant, yet completely honest, positive affirmations. "Yes, you are amazing, but let's talk about someone else for a change!"

2. **Empathy Emulator:** Struggling with empathy? EgoTamer's Empathy Emulator provides real-time prompts to help navigate conversations. "Now would be a great time to ask how they're doing and actually listen!"

3. **Compliment Counter:** Keeping track of compliments received versus given can be hard. EgoTamer's Compliment Counter ensures balance: "You've received 42 compliments today. Time to give one back!"

4. **Selfie Limiter**: For those prone to excessive selfie-taking, EgoTamer's Selfie Limiter steps in: "You've hit your selfie quota for the day. Time to focus on the world outside your camera!"

5. **Reality Check**: When grandiose fantasies start to take over, EgoTamer's Reality Check feature delivers a gentle nudge: "Winning a Nobel Prize for organizing your sock drawer? Let's aim a bit more realistically."

6. **Audience Simulator**: Missing an audience for your stories? EgoTamer's Audience Simulator listens to every tale with rapt attention and even throws in a standing ovation, ensuring you feel heard without overwhelming real-life friends.

With EgoTamer 3000, managing narcissism has never been more...entertaining. Because sometimes, even the biggest egos need a little AI assistance!

In summary, the integration of AI in managing narcissism is driven by its ability to make life easier, promote autonomy, and provide constant support, addressing key challenges in the treatment of NPD.

Benefits of AI in Mental Health for Individuals with NPD

The integration of Artificial Intelligence (AI) into mental healthcare offers several potential benefits for individuals with Narcissistic Personality Disorder (NPD), as well as for those treating and supporting them. These benefits span from improved diagnostic processes to personalized treatment plans. Here are some key areas where AI can make a significant impact:

1. Enhanced Diagnostic Tools

AI can analyze vast amounts of data from clinical interviews, psychological tests, and even patterns in social media use to assist in diagnosing NPD more accurately. This can lead to earlier intervention and treatment.

2. Personalized Treatment Plans

By analyzing data from a variety of sources, including patient history and treatment outcomes, AI can help in developing highly personalized treatment plans that may be more effective for the individual's specific manifestation of NPD.

3. Monitoring and Feedback

AI-powered applications can monitor the user's behavior and mood, providing real-time feedback and strategies to manage symptoms. For individuals with NPD, this can include prompts for reflection on interpersonal interactions or reminders to practice empathy.

4. Accessible Therapeutic Tools

AI can deliver therapeutic content and exercises through chatbots or virtual therapists, making mental health support more accessible. This can be particularly useful for individuals with NPD who may initially be reluctant to seek help from human therapists due to stigma or a lack of insight into their condition.

5. Empathy and Social Improving Skills

There are AI-driven programs designed to help individuals recognize and interpret emotions in others, which can be beneficial for those with NPD in improving empathy and social skills.

6. Support for Therapists

AI can provide therapists with insights derived from data analysis, suggesting potential areas of focus or alerting them to the risk of adverse outcomes. This can enhance the therapeutic process for individuals with NPD by ensuring that interventions are timely and relevant.

7. Enhancing Engagement

Individuals with NPD might find AI-based interventions less judgmental and more engaging than traditional therapy, at least initially. This could increase their willingness to participate in treatment and self-improvement efforts.

8. Privacy and Anonymity-

For those concerned about privacy, AI-based tools can offer a degree of anonymity in the early stages of seeking help, potentially encouraging individuals to take the first steps toward treatment and support.

Apart from the above there are Top 5 (Tongue in cheek) Benefits of AI for Individuals with Narcissistic Personality Disorder.

1. Constant Validation On-Demand:

Need an ego boost at 3 AM? No problem! Your AI is always there to remind you how extraordinary you are. "Of course you're the smartest person in the room – even if it's a virtual room and you're the only one in it!"

2. Automated Applause:

Your AI comes equipped with an applause generator. Every time you make a comment, it delivers a round of applause.

Now you can finally get the standing ovation you deserve for finding your keys!

3. **Compliment Generator**:

Struggling to find someone who appreciates your greatness? AI has you covered with endless unique compliments. "You make even the most boring meetings feel like a TED Talk!"

4. **Empathy Emulator**:

Not your strong suit? No worries! Your AI can give you pointers. "Pro tip: Asking someone about their day makes them think you care. Go ahead, give it a try!"

5. **Personal PR Manager**:

Tired of tooting your own horn? Your AI can handle it. It'll subtly slip your achievements into conversations: "Did you know that [Your Name] just completed a Netflix marathon in record time?"

With AI, your brilliance will never go unnoticed again. Finally, a sidekick that truly understands and celebrates you – all day, every day!

Yes, the use of AI in mental healthcare for individuals with NPD holds promise for more precise diagnosis, personalized treatment, and greater accessibility to therapeutic resources. However, it's crucial to approach these technologies as complementary to human-delivered healthcare, rather than replacements, to ensure that the nuanced needs of each individual are met with empathy and understanding. As AI in mental health care evolves, it will be important to monitor outcomes and adjust approaches to maximize benefits for individuals with NPD and the broader mental health community.

Benefits of AI To Family Members

AI offers several benefits not just to individuals with Narcissistic Personality Disorder (NPD) but also to their family members. By providing tools, resources, and support, AI can help family members better understand NPD, manage their relationships, and take care of their own mental health. Here are some of the key benefits:

1. **Education and Awareness**

Informative Resources: AI-powered apps and platforms can offer educational materials about NPD, helping family members understand the disorder's nature, symptoms, and effects on behavior and relationships.

2. **Support Systems**

Digital Support Groups: AI can connect family members with online support groups or forums, providing a space to share experiences, advice, and support with others facing similar challenges.

3. **Stress Management**

Personalized Wellness Programs: AI applications can suggest personalized stress-reduction and wellness activities based on the user's preferences and needs, helping family members manage the emotional toll of dealing with NPD dynamics.

4. **Communication Assistance**

Improved Interaction Strategies: Through analyzing communication patterns, AI tools can offer suggestions for more effective ways of communicating with a loved one who has NPD, potentially reducing conflicts and misunderstandings.

5. Mental Health Monitoring

Early Warning Signs Detection: For family members struggling with their own mental health, AI-powered apps can monitor mood and stress levels, offering early detection of potential mental health issues and suggesting when to seek professional help.

6. Access to Therapy

Therapeutic Resources: AI chatbots and virtual therapy platforms can provide immediate, low-cost therapeutic interactions, offering coping strategies and emotional support to family members who may not have access to or the time for traditional therapy sessions.

7. Personalized Recommendations

Customized Care Strategies: Based on interactions and user data, AI can recommend personalized reading, activities, or exercises to help family members develop healthier coping mechanisms and improve their emotional intelligence and resilience.

8. Creating Boundaries

Guidance on Boundaries: AI tools can offer advice on setting and maintaining healthy boundaries with the narcissistic individual, a crucial step for family members trying to protect their mental health and well-being.

How AI Can Help Families Deal with Their Favorite Narcissist (In a lighter vein)

1. Praise Distributor:

Tired of showering compliments non-stop? Let AI take over! With the Praise Distributor, your AI can handle all the flattery: "Hey, your AI thinks you did a stellar job parking the car today. Gold medal performance!"

2. Conversation Steerer:

Need a break from their never-ending stories? The AI's Conversation Steerer gently redirects chats: "That's fascinating, but let's hear about someone else's day for a change!"

3. Reality Reminder:

When their delusions of grandeur get a bit too grand, the AI steps in with a gentle reality check: "Winning an Oscar for making breakfast? Let's just aim for perfectly scrambled eggs."

4. Empathy Trainer:

Encourage a little empathy with subtle hints from the AI: "Maybe ask Aunt Linda how her trip was. People usually enjoy talking about themselves too!"

5. Applause Breaks:

Whenever your family member does something mundane, like taking out the trash, the AI can provide an encouraging applause soundtrack. Who knew chores could be so celebrated?

6. **Social Buffer**:

Hosting a family event? The AI can serve as a buffer, engaging your favorite narcissist in deep conversation about their favorite topic – themselves – while everyone else sneaks off for a breather.

With AI's help, dealing with a narcissistic family member becomes a whole lot more manageable – and entertaining. Who knew technology could be so supportive and keep the peace, one automated compliment at a time?

Yes, while AI cannot replace the depth and empathy of human interactions, it can significantly supplement the support and resources available to family members of individuals with NPD. By leveraging AI for education, support, and personal wellness, family members can gain a stronger footing in navigating the complex dynamics of these relationships and maintaining their mental health.

Looking Ahead

Imagine AI as a quirky, tireless butler named Jeeves, dedicated to helping families manage the challenges of dealing with a narcissistic family member. Jeeves is always at your service, ready with witty responses and practical solutions.

For families, Jeeves offers a special app called "Narcissist Navigator." This app provides real-time advice on how to handle every grandiose proclamation and manipulative maneuver. When your narcissistic cousin starts boasting about their latest "unmatched" accomplishment, Jeeves sends you a calming notification: "Smile and nod, and remember, you're the real MVP for enduring this!"

Jeeves also excels in diffusing tension with humor. For instance, if a family member goes on a tirade about how no one appreciates their greatness, Jeeves might suggest replying with, "You're right, the Nobel Prize committee must have lost your number again."

Mental health professionals see Jeeves as their ultimate assistant. With a database of insightful strategies and a knack for pattern recognition, Jeeves helps therapists anticipate and counter the self-centered behaviors of narcissistic patients. Jeeves might even suggest therapeutic exercises like "mirror time," where the patient spends a few minutes a day complimenting their reflection—saving the therapist's energy for more productive sessions.

In the end, Jeeves becomes the unsung hero in both homes and therapy offices, providing just the right mix of empathy, humor, and practicality. Thanks to this AI butler, dealing with narcissistic personality disorder becomes a bit more manageable, and perhaps even a bit more amusing.

As we embark on this journey at the intersection of psychology and technology, let us approach the opportunities and challenges of AI with curiosity, humility, and a commitment to ethical practice. In the chapters that follow, we will explore specific AI-driven strategies for navigating narcissism, empowering individuals to embark on a path of self-discovery and personal transformation.

Chapter 3:
Self-Awareness

In this chapter, we delve into the transformative potential of AI-driven self-assessment tools for gaining insight into narcissistic personality patterns and fostering self-awareness. As we navigate the complexities of narcissism, we explore how technology can serve as a catalyst for introspection, reflection, and personal growth.

Why is Gaining Insight into Narcissistic Personality Patterns and Fostering Self-Awareness Important?

Imagine gaining insights into narcissistic personality patterns as if you're embarking on an Indiana Jones adventure, but instead of searching for ancient artifacts, you're uncovering the elusive treasure of self-awareness.

Your trusty AI sidekick, Robo-Jones, is there to guide you through the labyrinth of grandiosity and self-admiration.

Robo-Jones has a knack for spotting the telltale signs of narcissism, like a radar for finding over-inflated egos. When a narcissistic family member starts a monologue about their latest "world-changing" idea, Robo-Jones sends you a sly message: "Brace yourself, another legendary tale is about to unfold!"

To foster self-awareness in the narcissist, Robo-Jones introduces "The Mirror Quest." It's a fun and slightly mischievous game where the narcissist is gently nudged to look beyond their reflection. Robo-Jones might say, "Ever wondered what it's like to be as awesome as you? Try listening to others for a change—you might discover a world almost as interesting as yourself!"

Mental health professionals find Robo-Jones to be a secret weapon in their therapeutic arsenal. With witty reminders and insightful prompts, Robo-Jones helps narcissistic patients explore the concept of empathy. For example, it might suggest, "Imagine if everyone else had lives and feelings as complex as yours. Wild, right? Give it a shot and see what you find!"

As Robo-Jones leads the way with humor and a dash of sarcasm, navigating narcissistic personality patterns and fostering self-awareness becomes an adventurous journey. With each step, both family members and mental health professionals can uncover the hidden gems of empathy and self-reflection, making the path to understanding a bit more entertaining and rewarding.

Narcissistic Personality Disorder (NPD) is characterized by traits such as grandiosity, a need for admiration, and a lack of empathy. Gaining insight into these narcissistic personality patterns and fostering self-awareness is crucial for individuals with NPD. This awareness is essential for personal growth, improving relationships, and achieving effective treatment outcomes.

1. **Understanding Behavior:** Insight into narcissistic personality patterns allows individuals to recognize their behavioral tendencies, such as grandiosity, manipulation, and lack of empathy. This awareness enables them to understand how these patterns affect themselves and others.
2. **Improving Relationships:** Self-awareness helps narcissistic individuals recognize how their behavior impacts relationships. By fostering insight, they can develop empathy, acknowledge their impact on others, and work towards healthier interactions.
3. **Facilitating Growth:** Gaining insight into narcissistic traits and behaviors is crucial for personal development. It allows individuals to address underlying insecurities and vulnerabilities, fostering emotional growth and resilience.
4. **Treatment Efficacy:** In therapy, self-awareness enhances treatment efficacy by facilitating introspection and acceptance of flaws. It enables individuals to engage more effectively in therapeutic interventions and make meaningful progress towards recovery.
5. **Reducing Harm:** Fostering self-awareness helps prevent harm to oneself and others by reducing impulsive and destructive behaviors associated with

narcissistic tendencies. Individuals can learn to regulate their emotions and impulses more effectively.

Gaining insight into narcissistic personality patterns and fostering self-awareness is essential for personal growth, improving relationships, and effective treatment of narcissistic tendencies, ultimately leading to healthier and more fulfilling lives.

Empirically Supported Therapies for NPD and the Role of Self-Discovery and Self-Awareness

Empirically supported therapies for Narcissistic Personality Disorder (NPD) encompass a wide variety of approaches. Each of these modalities integrates self-awareness and self-discovery as fundamental components in treating NPD.

1. **Transference-Focused Psychotherapy (TFP):** TFP is empirically supported and focuses on understanding and managing intense emotions and relationships in NPD. It achieves this by encouraging individuals to explore their internal dynamics, fostering self-awareness, and facilitating insight into maladaptive patterns.
2. **Cognitive-Behavioral Therapy (CBT):** Another empirically supported therapy, CBT helps NPD individuals identify and challenge maladaptive thoughts and behaviors. Through self-discovery, individuals gain awareness of their cognitive distortions and develop healthier coping strategies.
3. **Psychodynamic Therapy:** Empirically validated, psychodynamic therapy delves into unconscious conflicts and early life experiences contributing to

NPD symptoms. By facilitating self-awareness and self-discovery, it enables individuals to gain insight into underlying issues and promote personal growth.
4. **Dialectical Behavior Therapy (DBT):** DBT, supported by evidence, teaches skills for emotional regulation and mindfulness. Through self-discovery, individuals enhance their awareness of emotions and behaviors, fostering improved interpersonal relationships and emotional stability.
5. **Schema Therapy:** Supported by research, schema therapy addresses core beliefs underlying NPD. Through self-discovery, individuals identify and challenge maladaptive schemas, promoting healthier ways of thinking, feeling, and behaving.
6. **SEHT** – Subconscious Energy Healing Therapy. Subconscious Energy Link Therapy taps into the hidden emotional currents, helping individuals with NPD connect with deeper, often overlooked feelings. This innovative approach fosters empathy and self-awareness by harmonizing subconscious energies. As a result, it gently redirects narcissistic tendencies towards healthier interpersonal dynamics.

These therapies collectively emphasize the importance of self-awareness and self-discovery in NPD treatment. They enable individuals to understand their internal dynamics, challenge maladaptive patterns, and cultivate healthier coping strategies and relationships, ultimately facilitating personal growth and recovery.

Willingness to Change and Narcissistic Personality Disorder (NPD)

Narcissistic Personality Disorder (NPD) presents a complex challenge when it comes to willingness to change. Individuals with NPD often exhibit traits such as grandiosity, a sense of entitlement, and a lack of empathy, which can hinder their receptiveness to change. However, despite the inherent difficulties, there is potential for growth and transformation with the right approach.

Understanding NPD and Resistance to Change

NPD is characterized by a pervasive pattern of grandiosity, need for admiration, and lack of empathy, which often leads to interpersonal difficulties and impairment in functioning. Individuals with NPD may struggle with self-awareness and have difficulty acknowledging their own shortcomings or the impact of their behavior on others. This lack of insight can contribute to resistance to change, as they may perceive themselves as flawless and believe they have nothing to improve upon.

Factors Influencing Willingness to Change

Several factors can influence an individual's willingness to change, including the severity of their NPD symptoms, their level of insight, and external motivators such as therapy or relationship dynamics. While some individuals with NPD may be resistant to change initially, others may be more open to the idea, particularly if they experience significant distress or negative consequences as a result of their behavior that have shown promise in treating NPD by addressing maladaptive beliefs and behaviors.

In conclusion, while willingness to change may present a significant challenge for individuals with NPD, it is not impossible. With the right support, therapy, and internal motivation, individuals with NPD can embark on a journey of self-discovery and growth. It is crucial for mental health professionals and loved ones to approach the process with patience, empathy, and understanding, recognizing that change is a gradual and complex process.

The Power of Self-Reflection- with AI self assessment tools

Self-reflection is a cornerstone of personal development, allowing individuals to gain insight into their thoughts, feelings, and behaviors. By examining our own experiences and motivations, we can identify patterns, uncover underlying beliefs, and make informed choices about our lives.

However, self-reflection can be a challenging and often daunting process, particularly when it comes to confronting aspects of ourselves that we may prefer to ignore or deny. This is where AI-driven self-assessment tools can play a valuable role, providing a structured and non-judgmental framework for exploring our own inner landscape.

AI-Driven Self-Assessment Tools- Assess yourself

AI-driven self-assessment tools leverage the power of machine learning algorithms to analyze vast amounts of data and identify patterns in human behavior. These tools can take various forms, including online quizzes, mobile apps, and virtual coaching platforms, each offering unique features and capabilities for self-discovery.

One example of an AI-driven self-assessment tool is the Narcissism Personality Inventory (NPI), which measures various dimensions of narcissism, including grandiosity, entitlement, and exhibitionism. By completing the NPI, individuals can gain insight into their own narcissistic tendencies and explore how these traits may impact their relationships and well-being.

Another example is the use of natural language processing (NLP) algorithms to analyze written text, such as journal entries or social media posts, for linguistic markers of narcissism. By examining patterns in language use, individuals can gain insight into their own self-expression and communication styles, uncovering hidden aspects of their personality.

AI Assisted Insights Leading To Personal Growth For Individuals With NPD

The concept of using AI to facilitate self-insight and personal growth in individuals with NPD or other mental health conditions is gaining interest globally. AI can offer personalized feedback, help track moods and behaviors, and provide therapeutic interventions, which can be particularly useful in a diverse and populous country like India, where mental health resources are often scarce or concentrated in urban areas.

The potential applications could include:

1. **AI-Powered Diagnostic Tools**: These can help in early identification of NPD traits, leading to timely intervention. By analyzing speech patterns, social media usage, and writing styles, AI could provide

insights into narcissistic traits, offering a starting point for self-awareness and growth.
2. **Virtual Reality (VR) and AI Therapies**: VR environments, guided by AI, can simulate social situations where individuals with NPD can practice empathy, understand different perspectives, and receive instant feedback on their responses. This could foster better social interactions and reduce narcissistic behaviors over time.
3. **AI-Driven Cognitive Behavioral Therapy (CBT)**: For individuals with NPD, AI can customize CBT techniques to address specific issues like lack of empathy, grandiosity, or vulnerability. By providing a safe, private space for reflection and learning, AI can facilitate the development of healthier thought patterns.
4. **Mood and Behavior Tracking Apps:** These apps can help individuals with NPD monitor their emotional states and behaviors, providing insights into triggers for narcissistic behaviors and suggesting strategies for managing them.

While specific studies from India focusing on AI's role in assisting individuals with NPD are not readily available, the country has a growing interest in leveraging technology for mental health. India's digital health initiatives and burgeoning tech industry suggest that research and application in this area may soon become more prevalent.

AI-Assisted Insights Leading To Professional Growth For Individuals With NPD

The potential for AI to assist in the professional growth of individuals with NPD, or indeed any individual, is significant. AI technologies, including machine learning algorithms, natural language processing, and predictive analytics, can offer personalized feedback, identify patterns in behavior and communication, and suggest areas for improvement. For individuals with NPD, such tools could be instrumental in highlighting and mitigating behaviors that may be detrimental in professional settings, such as difficulties in teamwork, challenges in accepting feedback, or issues with empathy.

Here are some ways AI could theoretically support professional growth in individuals with NPD:

1. **Feedback and Self-awareness**: AI tools can provide objective, non-judgmental feedback on communication styles and interpersonal interactions, which could help individuals recognize and adjust behaviors that may be perceived negatively by colleagues and superiors.
2. **Emotion Recognition and Regulation**: AI applications that analyze facial expressions, voice tone, and physiological responses can help individuals become more aware of their emotional reactions and learn to regulate emotions that could be disruptive in professional settings.
3. **Skill Development:** AI-driven educational platforms can customize learning paths to develop soft skills that are often challenging for individuals

with NPD, such as active listening, empathy, and collaboration.
4. **Performance Monitoring**: AI can track progress over time, offering insights into how changes in behavior are correlating with professional outcomes, reinforcing positive development and highlighting areas for ongoing improvement.
5. **Scenario-Based Training**: Through virtual reality or AI-simulated scenarios, individuals can practice responding to workplace situations, receive feedback, and refine their approach to leadership, negotiation, and conflict resolution.

Empowering Personal Growth

Ultimately, the goal of AI-driven self-assessment tools is to empower individuals to embark on a journey of self-discovery and personal growth. By providing feedback, insights, and resources for reflection, these tools enable individuals to gain a deeper understanding of themselves and their relationships, paving the way for positive change and transformation.

However, it is important to approach self-assessment with a spirit of openness, curiosity, and self-compassion. Rather than viewing narcissistic traits as fixed or immutable aspects of our identity, we can recognize them as opportunities for growth and learning, embracing the challenges and possibilities that they present.

How can friends and family navigate being around Patient of NPD who lacks self-awareness?

Navigating relationships with someone who has Narcissistic Personality Disorder (NPD) and lacks self-awareness can be challenging. Here are some strategies for friends and family:

1. **Educate Yourself**: Learn about NPD to understand the behavior patterns and dynamics.

2. **Set Boundaries**: Establish clear boundaries to protect your well-being and maintain emotional distance when necessary.

3. **Avoid Arguments**: Refrain from engaging in arguments or attempting to change the person's behavior, as this often leads to further conflict.

4. **Practice Self-Care**: Prioritize self-care by engaging in activities that promote your mental and emotional well-being.

5. **Seek Support**: Surround yourself with trusted friends, family members, or support groups who can offer understanding and validation.

6. **Maintain Realistic Expectations**: Accept that you may not be able to change the person with NPD and focus on managing your own reactions and expectations.

7. **Practice Empathy**: While it may be challenging, try to empathize with the person's struggles and recognize that their behavior stems from underlying insecurities.

8. **Seek Professional Help**: Consider seeking guidance from a therapist or counselor who can provide personalized strategies and support for coping with the challenges of interacting with someone with NPD.

By implementing these strategies, friends and family can navigate their relationships with individuals with NPD who lack self-awareness while prioritizing their own well-being.

How AI and other technological tools can can help friends and family of NPD patients who lack self-awareness. and how these tools can make their lives better

AI and technology offer innovative solutions to support friends and family of NPD patients who lack self-awareness in several ways:

1. **Online Support Groups**: AI-powered platforms can connect individuals with similar experiences, providing a supportive community where friends and family can share advice and coping strategies

2. **Virtual Therapeutic Tools**: AI-driven therapy apps can offer guided exercises and psychoeducation to help friends and family better understand NPD and learn effective communication and boundary-setting techniques.

3. **Emotion Recognition Software**: AI can analyze facial expressions and vocal tone to detect emotions, helping friends and family recognize subtle cues and respond empathetically .

4. **Personalized Resources**: AI algorithms can curate personalized resources and educational materials tailored to the specific needs and challenges faced by friends and family members of NPD patients.
5. **24/7 Support Chatbots**: AI-powered chatbots can provide immediate support and guidance, offering coping strategies and reassurance to friends and family members whenever they need it.
6. **Teletherapy Services**: AI-enabled teletherapy platforms can connect friends and family with mental health professionals for remote counseling sessions, offering convenient access to support and guidance.

By leveraging AI and technology, friends and family of NPD patients can access valuable resources, support networks, and tools to navigate the challenges of supporting their loved ones while also prioritizing their own well-being.

Embracing AI for Self-Awareness and NPD Management: A Call to Innovate

The intersection of AI and mental health presents an unparalleled opportunity to revolutionize the management of Narcissistic Personality Disorder (NPD) with a focus on enhancing self-awareness. This initiative calls upon entrepreneurs, researchers, and institutions to spearhead the integration of AI in NPD management, fostering significant professional and personal growth for individuals affected by the disorder.

Why Focus on AI, Self-Awareness, and NPD?

AI holds immense potential in diagnosing, treating, and managing NPD by promoting self-awareness. This self-awareness is crucial for individuals with NPD to understand and modify their behaviors positively. AI-driven therapeutic solutions can address the unique challenges faced by NPD patients, improving their quality of life and enhancing their interpersonal relationships and professional achievements.

Opportunities for Innovation

1. **Tech Startups**: Innovators are encouraged to develop AI-driven platforms that offer real-time support and personalized therapy for NPD patients, focusing on self-awareness and behavioral modifications. Potential features include virtual reality therapy, AI-based assessment tools, and interactive self-help apps.

2. **Academic Research**: Scholars can engage in groundbreaking studies to explore the effectiveness of AI in treating NPD by enhancing self-awareness. Research areas include AI algorithms for early diagnosis, predictive analytics for therapy outcomes, and the development of empathetic AI models.

3. **Government Initiatives**: Policymakers and institutions can advocate for and participate in government-funded projects aimed at integrating AI into mental health care, emphasizing self-awareness. These initiatives can support large-scale implementation and ensure accessibility to advanced therapeutic solutions.

By joining this transformative journey, participants can create a positive impact on the lives of many, fostering both personal growth and professional success. Embrace the challenge and become a part of this innovative movement to improve the management of NPD through AI.

Simple and Do-able: Steps for NPD patients to Navigate and improve self-awareness:

For individuals with Narcissistic Personality Disorder (NPD), using technology and AI for self-awareness can be a constructive step. Here are some simple and doable action steps:

1. **Journaling Apps**: Encourage the use of journaling apps to track thoughts, feelings, and behaviors. Apps like Day One or Penzu provide a private space for reflection.

2. **Mood Tracking Apps**: Suggest using mood tracking apps like Moodpath or Daylio to monitor emotional fluctuations and identify patterns.

3. **Personality Assessments**: Recommend reputable personality assessment tools like the Myers-Briggs Type Indicator (MBTI) or the Big Five Personality Traits assessment. Discussing results with a therapist can provide insights.

4. **Feedback Tools**: Utilize feedback tools like 360-degree feedback surveys or anonymous feedback platforms to gain insights into how others perceive their behavior.

5. **Mindfulness Apps**: Encourage the use of mindfulness apps such as Headspace or Calm to practice self-reflection and emotional regulation.

6. **AI Chatbots**: Experiment with AI chatbots designed for mental health support. While they're not a substitute for professional therapy, they can offer insights and coping strategies.
7. **Self-Reflection Prompts**: Set reminders for self-reflection prompts throughout the day using smartphone apps or virtual assistants like Siri or Google Assistant.
8. **Online Support Communities**: Encourage participation in online support communities or forums where individuals with NPD can share experiences and learn from others.
9. **Digital Therapeutic Programs**: Explore digital therapeutic programs specifically designed for NPD or related issues, such as self-esteem building or assertiveness training.
10. **Regular Technology Breaks**: Encourage taking regular breaks from technology to engage in activities that promote self-awareness, such as meditation, nature walks, or creative pursuits.

It's important to remember that while technology and AI can be valuable tools for self-awareness, they should complement professional therapy and support, not replace it. Encourage individuals with NPD to work closely with mental health professionals to develop a comprehensive treatment plan. By incorporating these additional points, individuals with NPD can leverage technology and AI in diverse ways to enhance their self-awareness and overall well-being. Not all points listed above directly involve AI components.

While some points, like AI chatbots and emotion recognition tools, specifically incorporate artificial intelligence technology, others focus more on utilizing digital tools, online platforms, or virtual reality without necessarily relying on AI. By incorporating these AI-based tools into their self-awareness and self-discovery journey, NPD patients can access innovative resources to support their personal growth and development.

Case study: Narcissistic Tendencies- Jai's Story of Realization and Recovery

Introduction

Jai, a 35-year-old man, seemed to have it all—charisma, intelligence, and an impressive resume. Yet beneath this veneer of success lay a troubled individual struggling with Narcissistic Personality Disorder (NPD). His early life was marred by parental neglect and emotional abuse, fostering deep-seated insecurities and a slew of maladaptive personality traits.

Early Struggles

Jai's childhood was anything but nurturing. With parents who were either absent or emotionally abusive, he grew up feeling insignificant and unloved. To cope, Jai developed a facade of grandiosity, constantly boasting about his accomplishments and belittling others to feel superior. This behavior seeped into his adult life, straining relationships and making him difficult to work with.

At work, Jai's sense of entitlement and need for admiration caused frequent conflicts. He expected special treatment and resented any form of criticism, often leading to heated arguments with colleagues and superiors. His personal relationships were similarly fraught, characterized by cycles of intense idealization followed by harsh devaluation. Jai's partners found him charming at first, but his lack of empathy and constant need for validation quickly became overwhelming.

The Turning Point

Despite the outward display of confidence, Jai's self-esteem was fragile. Each failure or critique hit him hard, triggering intense emotional reactions and defensiveness. It wasn't until a particularly devastating breakup and a series of professional setbacks that Jai began to see the pattern. He realized that his life was falling apart, and he was the common denominator.

A friend suggested therapy, but Jai was initially resistant. Admitting he had a problem felt like a blow to his ego. However, as his isolation grew, so did his desperation for change. Reluctantly, he scheduled his first appointment with a therapist specializing in NPD.

The Role of Self-Awareness and Self-Discovery

Therapy was a revelation for Jai. Through sessions of Cognitive-Behavioral Therapy (CBT), Dialectical Behavior Therapy (DBT), and Schema Therapy, Jai began to peel back the layers of his personality. He started to see how his childhood experiences had shaped his behaviors and how these behaviors were sabotaging his life.

One of the most significant breakthroughs came from developing self-awareness. Jai learned to recognize his narcissistic tendencies—his grandiosity, entitlement, and lack of empathy. This self-awareness was painful but necessary. It allowed him to understand the impact of his actions on others and himself, providing the motivation to change.

Incorporating AI and Technology

Although AI wasn't initially part of Jai's therapy, its incorporation could have significantly enhanced his treatment and recovery process. Various AI techniques could have been used to help Jai manage his Narcissistic Personality Disorder (NPD). For instance, AI-based assessment tools could analyze Jai's speech and behavior patterns, providing real-time feedback during therapy sessions. This would enable both Jai and his therapist to identify areas needing attention and track improvements accurately. Virtual Reality (VR) therapy could simulate real-life social scenarios, allowing Jai to practice interpersonal skills and empathetic responses in a controlled setting. This immersive experience would help him develop better social interactions and reduce narcissistic tendencies by managing real-life situations safely.

Moreover, AI-driven self-reflection apps could offer personalized self-reflection exercises, journaling prompts, and mindfulness practices, enhancing Jai's self-awareness and insight by encouraging regular introspection and providing tailored feedback based on his progress and needs. Advanced machine learning models could predict the onset of narcissistic behaviors by analyzing structural and behavioral data, helping anticipate and mitigate potential issues before they escalate. These models would provide proactive intervention strategies tailored to Jai's specific patterns.

Furthermore, utilizing machine learning techniques to uncover neural pathways linked to narcissism can offer deeper insights into Jai's condition. Understanding the neural basis of his behavior would allow for more targeted and effective therapeutic approaches. By integrating these AI technologies, Jai's therapy could have been more personalized, efficient, and effective, ultimately accelerating his journey toward recovery and personal growth.

The Fight for Recovery

Recovery was not a linear process. Jai faced many setbacks and moments of doubt. However, he persevered dispite it all. He practiced mindfulness to stay present and connected with his emotions, sought feedback from trusted friends, and kept a journal to track his progress.

Gradually, Jai began to see improvements. He developed empathy, improved his relationships, and found healthier ways to cope with stress. He learned to set boundaries, respect others' limits, and take responsibility for his actions.

Therapy became a cornerstone of his life, providing ongoing support and guidance.

A Happier Life

Jai's journey was long and arduous, but it led him to a place of genuine happiness and fulfillment. By confronting his narcissistic traits and working tirelessly to change, he transformed his life. His relationships flourished, his career stabilized, and he found a sense of peace that had eluded him for so long.

Conclusion

Jai's story is a testament to the power of self-awareness and the importance of seeking help. His struggle with Narcissistic Personality Disorder was challenging, but with the right support and a commitment to change, he overcame his inner demons. Jai's journey highlights the potential of combining traditional therapy with advanced AI technologies to enhance mental health treatment, offering hope to others facing similar battles.

In the chapters that follow, we will explore specific AI-driven strategies for navigating narcissism, building on the foundation of self-awareness and reflection established in this chapter. Together, let us harness the power of technology to embark on a journey of self-discovery and personal transformation.

Chapter 4:
From Awareness to Action: Implementing AI Strategies for Behavioural Change

In this chapter, we transition from introspection to action, exploring how AI-driven strategies can be implemented to address narcissistic personality patterns and facilitate meaningful personal growth. As we navigate the complexities of narcissism, we delve into practical techniques and tools that empower individuals to translate self-awareness into positive change.

What does it mean to move from self awareness to real change?

Moving from self-awareness to genuine change involves translating insights from introspection into concrete actions and behavioral modifications. Self-awareness serves as the cornerstone of meaningful transformation by facilitating an understanding of one's thoughts, emotions, and actions. True change materializes when individuals utilize this awareness to pinpoint areas for enhancement and actively pursue personal growth.

This process encompasses acknowledging strengths and weaknesses, establishing objectives, and consistently progressing towards self-improvement. Embracing discomfort and confronting entrenched habits are fundamental components of this transformative journey. Ultimately, effecting real change demands dedication, resilience, and a readiness to adopt fresh perspectives and behaviors for a more enriching life.

Transitioning from self-awareness to positive change necessitates comprehending one's inner workings and employing this understanding to foster advancement and better relationships. It entails recognizing areas for growth and actively striving to bolster personal well-being. Practical methods to facilitate this transition include mindfulness practices, like meditation and self-reflection exercises, which promote present-moment awareness.

Additionally, journaling serves as a potent tool for introspection, enabling individuals to delve into their thoughts and emotions, thereby enhancing self-awareness. Seeking feedback from trusted sources and utilizing self-assessment tools offer valuable external viewpoints and insights into areas ripe for development. By integrating these strategies into daily life, individuals can harness the potency of self-awareness to catalyze positive change and personal development.

However, individuals grappling with Narcissistic Personality Disorder (NPD) face unique challenges that complicate this journey. Further exploration of these challenges will be addressed in the subsequent sections.

Need for Exploring Strategies to Address Narcissistic Personality Patterns and Facilitate Meaningful Personal Growth

Narcissistic Personality Disorder (NPD) presents significant challenges for both those affected and the people around them. Transitioning from introspection to actionable strategies is vital in managing and mitigating the adverse effects of narcissistic behaviors. While recognizing and understanding these traits through introspection is an important first step, turning self-awareness into actionable change remains a significant challenge for many individuals with NPD.

Self-awareness is the cornerstone of personal growth for individuals with NPD. Acknowledging and accepting narcissistic tendencies as part of one's identity is essential for initiating change. However, self-awareness alone is not enough without the willingness to engage in corrective actions. This process involves understanding the impact of one's behavior on others and recognizing the necessity for change. A core deficit in NPD is the lack of empathy. Therapeutic interventions often aim to foster empathy by encouraging individuals to understand and consider others' perspectives. Techniques such as role-playing and empathy training exercises can help individuals with NPD develop greater compassion and interpersonal sensitivity.Integrating these strategies into daily life is crucial for sustained personal growth for individuals with NPD.

Empathy and NPD

Cognitive and Emotional Empathy

Cognitive empathy refers to the ability to understand another person's perspective, while emotional empathy involves sharing and responding to another's emotional state. Empirical studies have shown that individuals with NPD display significant deficits in both types of empathy. Ritter et al. (2011) conducted a study assessing cognitive and emotional empathy in patients with NPD and found a pronounced lack of both cognitive and emotional empathy compared to control groups.

Variability in Empathic Functioning

Despite the general deficits, there is variability in empathic functioning among individuals with NPD. Baskin-Sommers et al. (2014) highlighted this variability through case studies, demonstrating that some individuals with NPD might show situational or selective empathy based on personal interests or gains. This selective empathy is often manipulative, aimed at maintaining their grandiose self-image.

Understanding the challenge of behavior change in an NPD patient is like trying to teach a cat to fetch – theoretically possible, but hilariously unpredictable. You might find yourself thinking, "Is today the day they realize the world doesn't revolve around them?" It's a rollercoaster ride where every small breakthrough feels like discovering fire, only for the next ego flare-up to leave you wondering if they've ever even seen a spark.

Understanding the Challenges of Behavioral Change in NPD Patients

Narcissistic Personality Disorder (NPD) presents unique challenges in facilitating behavioral change. Individuals with NPD often exhibit entrenched patterns of behavior and thought that can be resistant to modification. Here, we delve into the complexities surrounding behavioral change in NPD patients and explore the obstacles that clinicians and patients face in this process.

1. Poor Boundaries

NPD patients typically struggle with maintaining healthy boundaries in relationships, which can impede therapeutic progress. Their inflated sense of self-importance and disregard for others' needs can lead to difficulties in forming genuine connections and fostering trust with therapists.

2. Ambivalence About Change

Many NPD patients exhibit ambivalence towards the prospect of change. While they may recognize the consequences of their behavior, they may also resist interventions that challenge their self-perception or require them to confront underlying insecurities. This ambivalence can manifest as resistance to therapy or a lack of engagement in treatment.

3. Alliance Challenges

Establishing a therapeutic alliance with NPD patients can be particularly challenging due to their conflicted sense of grandiosity and vulnerability. Clinicians may struggle to navigate power dynamics and maintain rapport while addressing the patient's deep-seated insecurities and defenses.

4. Resistance to Vulnerability

NPD patients often resist vulnerability and emotional exposure, viewing such experiences as threats to their self-image. This reluctance to engage in introspection or disclose authentic emotions can hinder progress in therapy and limit opportunities for meaningful behavioral change.

Overcoming Challenges

In conclusion, while the challenges of facilitating behavioral change in NPD patients are significant, they are not insurmountable. With patience, understanding, and evidence-based interventions, clinicians can support NPD patients on their journey towards healing and self-discovery.

Therapy and Behavioural Change in NPD patients

Empirically sound therapies for Narcissistic Personality Disorder (NPD) encompass various approaches aimed at facilitating behavioral change in affected individuals. Cognitive-Behavioral Therapy (CBT) targets maladaptive thought patterns and behaviors by challenging distorted beliefs associated with NPD, fostering realistic perceptions of self and others. Psychoanalytic therapy delves into underlying causes of NPD, often rooted in childhood experiences, fostering self-awareness and insight.

Dialectical Behavior Therapy (DBT) equips individuals with practical skills to manage distressing emotions and navigate interpersonal conflicts more effectively, leading to healthier behaviors and relationships. Schema Therapy targets core beliefs and maladaptive schemas underlying NPD, promoting emotional regulation and interpersonal skills. SEHT – subconscious energy healing therapy taps into their subconscious mind to facilitate behaviour change.

These therapies facilitate change by increasing self-awareness, challenging maladaptive beliefs, and developing coping skills. By exploring past experiences and behaviors, individuals with NPD gain insight into their patterns of thinking and relating to others, fostering meaningful behavioral change over time.

Through these therapeutic approaches, individuals with NPD can gradually modify maladaptive behaviors, develop more adaptive coping strategies, and cultivate self-awareness, ultimately leading to improved interpersonal relationships and overall well-being.

Identifying Maladaptive Patterns

The first step in addressing narcissistic tendencies is to identify maladaptive patterns of thinking, feeling, and behaving.

Strategies for identifying maladaptive behavioral patterns in individuals with Narcissistic Personality Disorder (NPD) involve various approaches. Firstly, observing interpersonal dynamics can reveal patterns of manipulation, exploitation, and a lack of empathy in relationships, which are hallmark traits of NPD. Secondly, assessing reactions to criticism, such as extreme defensiveness or rage, can indicate fragile self-esteem commonly associated with NPD. Additionally, evaluating grandiose behaviors, like exaggerated self-importance and fantasies of success, helps identify narcissistic tendencies.

Monitoring maladaptive coping mechanisms, such as denial or blaming others for failures, can also shed light on dysfunctional behaviors. Furthermore, reviewing behaviors across different settings, including work and social environments, aids in identifying consistent maladaptive patterns.

Lastly, assessing power dynamics in relationships, such as attempts to dominate conversations, can highlight narcissistic traits. These strategies enable early recognition of maladaptive behaviors associated with NPD, facilitating tailored interventions and treatment approaches.

Patients with Narcissistic Personality Disorder (NPD) can engage in self-assessment of maladaptive behavioral patterns through the following steps:

1. **Reflection:** Take time to reflect on past interactions and behaviors in various situations, such as relationships, work, and social settings. Consider how these behaviors may have impacted others and examine any recurring themes or patterns.

2. **Honesty:** Practice honesty with oneself by acknowledging the presence of narcissistic traits or behaviors. This may involve admitting to moments of grandiosity, a lack of empathy, or difficulties in maintaining healthy relationships.

3. **Comparison:** Compare personal behaviors and reactions to typical responses in similar situations.

Evaluate whether your responses align with healthy and adaptive behaviors or if they veer towards maladaptive patterns associated with NPD.

4. **Feedback:** Seek feedback from trusted individuals, such as friends, family, or mental health professionals, regarding your behavior and its impact on them. Listen openly to their perspectives and consider their insights without becoming defensive.

5. **Journaling:** Keep a journal to record thoughts, emotions, and behaviors regularly. Reviewing journal entries can provide valuable insights into recurring patterns, triggers for maladaptive behaviors, and progress over time.

6. **Self-Examination:** Engage in introspection to explore the underlying motivations behind behaviors associated with NPD. Consider any insecurities, fears of inadequacy, or childhood experiences that may contribute to these patterns.

By actively engaging in self-assessment, individuals with NPD can gain greater insight into their maladaptive behavioral patterns, paving the way for personal growth, and the development of healthier coping mechanisms

Aiding NPD patients using AI for identifying and changing maladaptive behavioral patterns:

1. **Behavioral Analysis**: AI can analyze vast datasets, including speech patterns and online interactions, to detect maladaptive behaviors.

2. **Early Intervention:** AI can facilitate early intervention by recognizing patterns indicative of NPD and alerting individuals or healthcare providers

3. **Personalized Therapy**: AI-driven therapy tools can offer personalized interventions tailored to the specific needs of NPD patients, helping them recognize and modify maladaptive behaviors

4. **Virtual Reality Exposure**: Virtual reality environments can simulate social interactions, allowing NPD patients to observe their behavior and its effects on others, fostering self-awareness and facilitating behavioral change

   4. **Cognitive Behavioral Therapy (CBT) Apps**: Mobile applications powered by AI algorithms can deliver CBT-based interventions, guiding NPD patients through exercises aimed at challenging maladaptive beliefs and behaviors
   5. **SEHT** – Subconscious Energy Healing therapies using power of visualizations can also positively impact and help in personal growth.

AI-driven self-assessment tools offer valuable feedback and insights into individuals' behaviors, aiding in understanding the roots of narcissistic tendencies. These tools analyze patterns like grandiosity and lack of empathy, facilitating self-awareness and prompting proactive change. Armed with this understanding, individuals can challenge maladaptive behaviors, fostering healthier relationships. Furthermore, AI and technology provide timely support and tailored interventions for NPD patients, aiding in effective pattern correction and personal growth.

Setting Goals for Change

Once maladaptive patterns have been identified, the next step is to set goals for change.

Goal Setting Process for NPD Patients:

Setting goals for NPD patients is like drafting a plan for world domination but with a twist of reality. Instead of aiming to be crowned "Supreme Ruler of the Universe," we start with more modest goals, like "Listen to someone else's story without interrupting." Each goal feels like negotiating with a celebrity: "Sure, you can talk about your latest 'achievement,' but first, let's practice asking others how their day was—without turning it into a monologue about yours!"

Some specific pointers may be as follows ;

1. **Write down the Maladaptive Behavior**: Clearly articulate the maladaptive behavior, such as seeking excessive admiration or lacking empathy, and acknowledge its impact on relationships and personal well-being.

2. **Understand Consequences**: List the negative consequences of the behavior, including strained relationships, loneliness, and dissatisfaction with oneself and others.

3. **Envision Future Consequences**: Consider the potential future outcomes if the behavior remains unchanged, imagining a life filled with continued interpersonal difficulties and emotional distress.

4. **Reflect on Desired Future**: Reflect on whether the current trajectory aligns with personal values and

goals, and whether changes are necessary to achieve a more fulfilling future.

5. **Desire Change**: If the current path is undesirable, envision a future characterized by healthier relationships, improved self-esteem, and greater emotional resilience.

6. **Define Positive Traits**: Describe the characteristics, values, and behaviors of individuals with healthy self-esteem and empathy, and recognize the importance of cultivating these traits.

7. **Incorporate Positive Traits**: Identify specific positive traits and behaviors that can be developed and integrated into daily life to facilitate personal growth and positive change.

8. **Establish Future Vision**: Visualize how life will look and feel once these changes are implemented, focusing on increased satisfaction, fulfillment, and genuine connections with others.

Challenges Faced by NPD Patients in Goal Setting and How to Overcome Them:

Navigating goal-setting with NPD patients is like trying to teach a peacock to be humble—it's a colorful challenge. We start by gently reminding them that the world won't implode if they're not the center of attention for five minutes. It's a bit like convincing a Kardashian to give up selfies—possible, but requires a delicate balance of humor and persuasion. So, we trade "I am the best" affirmations for "I am working on not interrupting people to talk about myself" mantras. Baby steps, folks, baby steps. Some of these issues are :

- **Resistance to Change**: NPD patients may resist acknowledging their maladaptive behaviors and the need for change. Overcoming this requires a willingness to engage in self-reflection and therapy, where they can explore underlying issues and motivations.
- **Maintaining Motivation**: Sustaining motivation for long-term change can be challenging. Setting small, achievable goals, seeking social support, and celebrating progress can help maintain motivation.
- **Self-Esteem Issues**: NPD patients may struggle with low self-esteem beneath their grandiose facade. Building self-compassion and self-acceptance through therapy and self-care practices can address this challenge.

The family plays a significant role in supporting NPD patients during the goal-setting

Lets look into it.

1. **Understanding and Acceptance**: Family members can provide a supportive environment by understanding the challenges associated with NPD and accepting the individual despite their condition.
2. **Encouragement and Motivation**: Family support can motivate NPD patients to engage in goal-setting activities and pursue positive changes in their behavior and attitudes.
3. **Setting Boundaries**: By establishing clear and healthy boundaries, family members can guide NPD patients in understanding appropriate behaviors and interactions, facilitating goal achievement.
4. **Providing Feedback**: Constructive feedback from family members can help NPD patients gain insight into their behaviors and their impact on others, aiding in the goal-setting process.
5. **Modeling Healthy Behaviors**: Family members can serve as role models by demonstrating healthy coping mechanisms and interpersonal skills, which NPD patients can emulate in their goal-setting journey.

Overall, the family's support, understanding, and active participation are vital for NPD patients in setting and achieving their goals for personal growth and recovery.

AI based tools help NPD patients in goal setting:

AI-driven tools play a crucial role in assisting NPD patients with goal setting by leveraging advanced technologies to provide tailored support:

1. **Data Analysis**: Analyzing extensive data helps identify behavioral patterns and trends, aiding in personalized goal setting.
2. **Predictive Modeling**: Predicting outcomes of different strategies helps NPD patients make informed decisions, fostering effective goal setting.
3. **Personalized Recommendations**: Offering customized recommendations based on individual characteristics enhances goal-setting strategies.
4. **Feedback and Monitoring**: Real-time feedback and progress monitoring enable NPD patients to track improvement and adjust strategies accordingly.
5. **Virtual Support**: Virtual systems provide continuous engagement, offering reminders and motivation to stay committed to goals.
6. **Customized Interventions**: Tailored interventions address specific challenges, optimizing the goal-setting process for NPD patients.

AI-driven tools, through their multifaceted capabilities, empower NPD patients to set and achieve meaningful goals, facilitating their journey towards personal growth and recovery.

Implementing Behavior Change Strategies

With goals in place, the next step is to implement behavior change strategies aimed at fostering personal growth and development.

Implementing behavioral change in individuals diagnosed with Narcissistic Personality Disorder (NPD)

Implementing behavioral change in individuals diagnosed with Narcissistic Personality Disorder (NPD) necessitates a tailored approach targeting their maladaptive behavioral patterns. Here are strategies for NPD patients to enact behavioral change:

1. **Recognition of the Need for Change:** NPD patients must acknowledge the adverse effects of their maladaptive behaviors on themselves and those around them. This acknowledgment serves as the initial step toward initiating change. For instance, recognizing how their need for constant admiration may strain relationships.

2. **Prioritization of Behaviors:** It's crucial to prioritize behaviors that significantly impact daily functioning and relationships. By focusing on addressing one behavior at a time, such as learning to accept constructive criticism without becoming defensive, patients can gradually make meaningful changes.

3. **Commitment to Change:** Making a conscious decision to actively engage in the process of behavioral change is essential. This involves understanding that change requires effort and dedication, like committing to attending therapy sessions regularly.

4. **Creation of an Action Plan:** Developing a detailed action plan outlining steps towards achieving goals is pivotal. Breaking down tasks into manageable actions, such as practicing active listening skills during conversations, facilitates progress.

5. **Gradual Implementation of Changes:** Starting with small changes in behavior and gradually expanding their scope over time is advisable. For instance, gradually reducing instances of interrupting others during discussions.

6. **Seeking Support:** Seeking guidance and encouragement from therapists, support groups, or mentors is beneficial. Being part of a supportive network can offer motivation and hold individuals accountable, like joining a group therapy session focused on improving interpersonal skills.

7. **Establishment of a Self-Reward System:** Celebrating progress and milestones achieved in behavioral change is crucial. Implementing a self-reward system, such as treating oneself to a favorite activity after successfully refraining from exhibiting narcissistic behaviors, can provide positive reinforcement.

8. **Practice and Feedback:** Regularly practicing new behaviors and soliciting feedback from others is essential. This feedback aids in identifying areas for improvement and reinforces positive changes, such as engaging in role-playing exercises with a therapist to practice empathy.

By adhering to these strategies, individuals with NPD can initiate and sustain meaningful behavioral change, leading to enhanced interpersonal relationships and overall well-being. It's essential to remember that change is attainable with dedication and effort

Role of AI in facilitating behavioural change in NPD patients:

AI-based technology can play a significant role in facilitating behavioral change in patients with Narcissistic Personality Disorder (NPD) by providing personalized support, enhancing self-awareness, and offering targeted interventions. Here's how AI can help and the various tools through which it can facilitate behavioral change:

1. **Virtual Therapy Assistants**: AI-powered chatbots and virtual assistants can offer round-the-clock support and guidance to individuals with NPD. These assistants can engage in conversations, provide coping strategies, and offer encouragement, thus supplementing traditional therapy.

2. **Behavioral Analysis Algorithms**: AI algorithms can analyze vast amounts of behavioral data to identify patterns and triggers associated with maladaptive behaviors in NPD patients. By recognizing these patterns, AI can help individuals gain insights into their behaviors and understand the underlying factors contributing to them.

3. **Personalized Intervention Recommendations**: Based on the analysis of behavioral data, AI can recommend personalized intervention strategies tailored to the specific needs and challenges of each NPD patient. These recommendations may include mindfulness exercises, cognitive-behavioral techniques, or communication skills training.

4. **Predictive Modeling**: AI can leverage predictive modeling techniques to anticipate potential relapses or setbacks in behavioral change efforts. By identifying high-risk situations, AI can provide timely interventions or alerts to help NPD patients stay on track with their treatment goals.
5. **Virtual Reality Therapy**: Virtual reality (VR) technology, combined with AI, can create immersive therapy environments for NPD patients. These VR simulations can replicate real-life scenarios, allowing individuals to practice coping strategies and interpersonal skills in a safe and controlled setting.
6. **Data-driven Feedback**: AI algorithms can analyze feedback from NPD patients and their caregivers to assess the effectiveness of behavioral change interventions. By continuously evaluating outcomes and adjusting strategies based on feedback, AI can optimize treatment approaches for better results.
7. **Mobile Applications**: AI-powered mobile applications can deliver on-the-go support and reminders to NPD patients, helping them stay engaged and motivated in their behavioral change journey. These apps may include features such as mood tracking, goal setting, and progress monitoring.

In conclusion, AI-based technology offers a wide range of tools and capabilities to support behavioral change in patients with NPD. From virtual therapy assistants to predictive modeling and VR therapy, these innovative solutions hold promise in enhancing self-awareness, providing personalized interventions, and improving treatment outcomes for individuals with NPD.

AI-driven coaching platforms can offer personalized advice, strategies, and resources for addressing specific areas of concern, such as emotional regulation, communication skills, and interpersonal relationships.

For example, individuals struggling with narcissistic tendencies may benefit from mindfulness practices aimed at cultivating self-awareness and empathy. AI-powered meditation apps can guide individuals through mindfulness exercises tailored to their specific needs and goals, providing support and encouragement along the way.

Monitoring Progress and Adjusting Strategies

As individuals embark on their journey of personal growth, it is important to monitor progress and adjust strategies as needed. Monitoring progress and adjusting strategies are crucial aspects of the behavioral change process as they ensure effectiveness and sustainability. Here's why it's important:

1. **Evaluation of Effectiveness**: Regularly monitoring progress allows individuals and practitioners to assess whether the chosen interventions are producing the desired outcomes. It provides valuable insights into what is working and what needs adjustment.

2. **Identification of Barriers**: Monitoring helps identify any obstacles or challenges that may hinder progress towards behavioral change goals. By

recognizing these barriers early on, appropriate strategies can be implemented to overcome them .

3. **Flexibility and Adaptability**: Behavioral change is a dynamic process influenced by various factors. Regular monitoring allows for flexibility in adjusting strategies based on individual needs, changing circumstances, or new insights .

4. **Motivation and Accountability**: Tracking progress provides individuals with a sense of accomplishment and motivation to continue their efforts towards change. It also holds them accountable for their actions and encourages adherence to the agreed-upon strategies.

5. **Optimization of Resources**: Monitoring progress helps optimize the allocation of resources by focusing on interventions that yield the best results. It ensures that time, effort, and resources are invested wisely in activities that contribute most effectively to behavioral change.

In summary, monitoring progress and adjusting strategies play a fundamental role in ensuring the success of behavioral change efforts by facilitating evaluation, adaptation, motivation, and resource optimization.

Proactive Steps for individuals with NPD :

Monitoring progress and adjusting strategies are crucial aspects of the behavioral change process for individuals with Narcissistic Personality Disorder (NPD) aiming to transition from maladaptive to healthy behavioral patterns. Here's how an NPD patient can play a proactive role in this process:

1. **Monitor Progress**:
    - Keep a journal: Regularly document thoughts, feelings, and behaviors to track changes over time.
    - Utilize self-assessment tools: Use validated assessments to objectively evaluate progress and identify areas needing improvement.

2. **Recognize Signs of Going Off Track**:
    - Increased self-centeredness or entitlement.
    - Difficulty empathizing with others.
    - Strained relationships due to narcissistic behaviors.

3. **Strategies to Get Back on Track**:
    - Practice self-reflection: Identify triggers and underlying emotions driving maladaptive behaviors.
    - Seek feedback: Consult with a therapist or trusted individuals to gain perspective and guidance.
    - Implement coping strategies: Engage in activities that promote emotional regulation and empathy, such as mindfulness or volunteering.

4. **Dealing with Emotions**:
    - Practice self-compassion: Acknowledge emotions without judgment and remind oneself that change is a gradual process.

- Utilize support systems: Lean on friends, family, or support groups for encouragement and validation.

5. **Adjusting Strategies**:
    - Flexibility: Be willing to modify strategies that are ineffective or exacerbate narcissistic traits.
    - Set realistic goals: Break down larger goals into smaller, achievable steps to maintain motivation and momentum.

6. **Course Correction**:
    - Evaluate progress regularly: Assess whether current strategies are yielding desired outcomes and adjust as needed.
    - Seek professional guidance: Consult with a therapist or mental health professional for additional support and guidance in navigating challenges and setbacks .

By actively monitoring progress, recognizing signs of regression, implementing appropriate coping strategies, and remaining open to adjustments, individuals with NPD can navigate the behavioral change process effectively and work towards healthier patterns of behavior.

When supporting an individual with Narcissistic Personality Disorder (NPD) in their journey towards behavioral change, family and friends play a crucial role. Here's how they can effectively contribute:

1. **Empathy and Understanding**:
   - Approach with empathy: Recognize that NPD is a complex mental health condition requiring understanding and patience.
   - Educate themselves: Learn about NPD to better understand the challenges the individual faces and the process of behavioral change.

2. **Encouragement and Support**:
   - Provide encouragement: Offer positive reinforcement and praise for progress, no matter how small.
   - Offer support: Be available to listen, provide emotional support, and assist with practical tasks when needed.

3. **Setting Boundaries**:
   - Establish healthy boundaries: Clearly communicate personal boundaries and expectations for behavior, while remaining firm and consistent.
   - Reinforce consequences: Enforce consequences for boundary violations to encourage accountability and respect.

4. **Self-Care**:
   - Prioritize self-care: Recognize the importance of maintaining one's own mental and emotional well-being.

- Seek support: Connect with support groups or seek therapy to navigate challenges and cope with stress associated with supporting an individual with NPD.

5. **Patience and Persistence**:

    - Practice patience: Understand that behavioral change takes time and setbacks may occur along the way.
    - Stay persistent: Maintain a supportive stance even during difficult moments, demonstrating commitment to the individual's well-being.

6. **Avoid Enabling**:

    - Avoid enabling behaviors: Refrain from reinforcing narcissistic traits or enabling unhealthy behaviors.
    - Encourage accountability: Hold the individual accountable for their actions and encourage them to take responsibility for their behavior.

By adopting an empathetic and supportive approach, setting healthy boundaries, prioritizing self-care, and maintaining patience and persistence, family and friends can play a significant role in facilitating the behavioral change process for individuals with NPD while safeguarding their own well-being.

Role of AI in Monitoring Progress and Adjusting Strategies

AI-based technology can play a significant role in supporting individuals with Narcissistic Personality Disorder (NPD) during the process of behavioral change, aiding their transition from maladaptive to healthy behavioral patterns. Here's how AI technology can help and the different tools available:

1. **Personalized Therapy**: AI-driven chatbots and virtual assistants can offer personalized therapy sessions tailored to the individual's needs [6]. These virtual platforms can provide continuous support, guidance, and feedback, helping NPD patients navigate their emotions and behaviors effectively.

2. **Behavioral Tracking**: AI-powered apps and wearable devices can track behavioral patterns and provide insights into triggers and trends [4]. By analyzing data such as mood fluctuations, social interactions, and daily activities, AI can identify patterns that contribute to maladaptive behaviors, enabling individuals to make informed changes.

3. **Cognitive Behavioral Therapy (CBT)**: AI algorithms can assist in delivering CBT-based interventions by identifying key beliefs and behaviors that contribute to dysregulation . These algorithms can generate personalized therapy plans and interventions targeting specific cognitive distortions and avoidance behaviors common in NPD.

4. **Sentiment Analysis**: AI tools can perform sentiment analysis on social media posts, service reviews, and feedback to gauge the emotional state and progress of individuals undergoing behavioral change. By monitoring sentiment trends, caregivers and clinicians can assess the effectiveness of interventions and adjust strategies accordingly.

5. **Virtual Support Groups**: AI-based platforms can facilitate virtual support groups and communities where individuals with NPD can connect with others facing similar challenges. These platforms offer a safe space for sharing experiences, receiving peer support, and learning coping strategies from others undergoing behavioral change.

6. **Predictive Analytics**: AI algorithms can analyze large datasets to predict outcomes of behavior change interventions. By leveraging historical data and individual characteristics, AI can forecast the likelihood of success for specific interventions, allowing clinicians to tailor treatment plans for optimal results.

In summary, AI-based technology offers a diverse range of tools and interventions to support NPD patients in their journey towards behavioral change. From personalized therapy sessions to behavioral tracking and predictive analytics, AI has the potential to revolutionize the way we approach and manage NPD, ultimately facilitating more effective treatment outcomes.

By regularly reviewing their progress and reflecting on their experiences, individuals can identify what is working well and what may need to be adjusted or modified. AI algorithms can analyze this data and provide personalized recommendations for optimizing behavior change strategies, ensuring that individuals stay on track towards their goals. AI-driven tracking tools can help individuals to track their behaviors, habits, and emotions over time, providing valuable feedback on their progress and areas for improvement.

Obstacles In Implementing AI Strategies For Personal Growth In Individuals With Npd

Implementing AI strategies for personal growth in individuals with Narcissistic Personality Disorder (NPD) presents unique challenges. While AI has the potential to offer significant benefits, such as personalized feedback and self-monitoring tools, there are several obstacles that need to be carefully managed:

1. **Lack of Insight**

- Individuals with NPD often have a limited insight into their own behaviors and how these behaviors affect others. This lack of self-awareness can make it difficult for AI strategies to be effective, as personal growth requires a degree of self-reflection and openness to feedback.

2. **Resistance to Feedback**

- A hallmark of NPD is sensitivity to criticism and a strong defensive reaction to perceived slights. AI systems that provide feedback on behaviors or suggest areas for improvement might be dismissed or met with hostility, especially if the feedback challenges the individual's self-perception.

3. Personalization Challenges

- AI systems rely on data to customize interventions and feedback. However, the complex nature of NPD, characterized by a wide range of symptoms and behaviors, can make it difficult to tailor AI strategies effectively. The AI system must be sophisticated enough to adapt to the nuanced needs of each individual.

4. Ethical and Privacy Concerns

- Implementing AI strategies involve collecting and analyzing personal data. There are significant ethical considerations and privacy concerns related to how this data is used, stored, and protected, especially in the context of mental health.

5. Technology Misuse

- There's a potential risk that individuals with NPD might misuse AI tools to reinforce their own perspectives or manipulate others, rather than engaging with these tools for genuine self-improvement.

6. Depersonalization of Therapy

- While AI can supplement therapeutic interventions, there's a risk that over-reliance on technology could depersonalize the therapy process. The therapeutic alliance between a therapist and their client is a critical component of treatment for NPD, and AI cannot replicate this relationship.

7. Access and Digital Literacy

- Access to technology and digital literacy can be significant barriers. Individuals without the skills to interact effectively with AI tools, or those without access to the necessary technology, may be excluded from these strategies for personal growth.

8. **Integration with Professional Care**

- Integrating AI strategies with ongoing professional care can be challenging. There needs to be a seamless connection between the insights generated by AI tools and the therapeutic processes guided by mental health professionals.

Overcoming These Obstacles

To overcome these obstacles, a multidisciplinary approach involving psychologists, AI developers, ethicists, and individuals with lived experience is necessary. Creating AI tools that are empathetic, ethical, and capable of handling the complexities of NPD, while also ensuring these tools are integrated thoughtfully into broader therapeutic practices, is crucial for their success in supporting personal growth in individuals with NPD.

Case Study: Unmasking Navya's Journey from Narcissism to Authenticity

Navya, a captivating 28-year-old woman, exuded confidence and success, drawing others to her with ease. However, beneath her confident exterior, Navya grappled with deep-seated issues stemming from her narcissistic tendencies.

Background:

Growing up in a competitive environment, Navya learned to prioritize achievement above all else. Her need for validation and admiration fueled her relentless pursuit of success, often at the expense of genuine connections.

Unveiling the Masks:

- ***Grandiosity:*** *Navya constantly sought recognition and praise, meticulously crafting a facade of triumph to feed her ego.*
- ***Empathy Void:*** *Her interactions lacked sincerity, functioning more as transactions than genuine emotional exchanges.*
- ***Fragile Armor:*** *Despite projecting an image of invincibility, Navya's self-esteem was fragile, easily shattered by criticism or rejection.*
- ***Relationship Turbulence:*** *Power struggles and manipulation characterized Navya's personal relationships, leaving behind a trail of broken connections.*

Turning Point:

After a string of failed relationships and conflicts at work, Navya reached a breaking point. Concerned friends intervened, urging her to seek therapy as a path to self-discovery.

Therapeutic Journey:

In therapy, Navya confronted the harsh realities of her behavior under the guidance of her therapist. Through introspection and self-reflection, she unraveled the intricate web of manipulation woven into her interactions.

Quest for Authenticity:

Recognizing the toxicity of her actions, Navya embarked on a journey towards authenticity. She understood that true fulfillment lay in genuine connections and inner peace, rather than external validation.

Behavioral Change:

With newfound self-awareness, Navya and her therapist worked collaboratively to implement change:

- ***Identifying Maladaptive Behaviors:*** *Navya learned to recognize and acknowledge her harmful patterns, laying the foundation for growth.*
- ***Setting Goals for Change:*** *She crafted a roadmap towards empathy and emotional regulation, striving to anchor her actions in authenticity.*
- ***Implementing Strategies:*** *Every step towards change was a deliberate act of defiance against her former self, a testament to her commitment to personal growth.*
- ***Monitoring Progress:*** *Navya tracked her evolution, celebrating successes and adjusting her approach in the face of setbacks.*

Challenges and Triumphs:

Navya's journey was fraught with challenges and moments of doubt. However, with the support of her therapist and loved ones, she persevered, using each stumble as an opportunity for growth.

Embracing Authenticity:

Through resilience and self-reflection, Navya emerged from her struggles, shedding the cloak of narcissism that once defined her. She found solace in genuine connections, embracing her vulnerabilities as sources of strength.

Impactful Transformation:

Navya's transformation radiated beyond her own life, inspiring others to embark on their own journeys of self-discovery. In embracing authenticity, she found a sense of fulfillment and purpose, paving the way for a brighter future for herself and those around her.

In the chapters that follow, we will explore specific AI-driven techniques and interventions for addressing narcissistic personality patterns and promoting personal growth. By harnessing the power of technology and taking proactive steps towards change, individuals can embark on a journey of transformation and self-discovery that transcends the limitations of narcissism.'

Chapter 5:
Overcoming Narcissistic Challenges: AI-Driven Techniques for Emotional Regulation

Navigating narcissistic challenges with AI-driven techniques for emotional regulation can be a humorous journey. Imagine AI tools like a daily compliment dispenser to satisfy validation needs, or a bot that gently redirects self-obsessed monologues. An empathy emulator could simulate others' feelings, while a humility helper subtly encourages modesty. Validation valets offer automated praise for small acts, and deflation stations bring overinflated egos back to earth. Sarcasm sentinels teach the art of taking a joke, and gratitude gurus guide towards appreciation over self-admiration. With these playful tools, even the most self-absorbed can balance self-love with humility and empathy.

In this chapter, we delve into the unique challenges that individuals with narcissistic tendencies face in regulating their emotions and managing interpersonal relationships. Drawing upon the insights of psychology and the capabilities of artificial intelligence, we explore innovative techniques and strategies for overcoming these challenges and fostering emotional well-being.

Understanding Emotions

Emotions are like the colorful cast of a sitcom in your brain. Here's a humorous take on them:

1. Joy: The bubbly character who finds sunshine on the gloomiest days, always wearing a smile like it's going out of fashion.

2. Sadness: The melancholy poet of the group, who makes everything feel like a rainy day, even at the beach.

3. Anger: The fiery hothead who flips the table when their coffee isn't hot enough, but calms down quickly with a good hug or a piece of chocolate.

4. Fear: The skittish friend who jumps at their own shadow and insists on a safety drill for everything, including opening mail.

5. Disgust: The snooty critic who turns their nose up at anything less than perfection, from bad manners to questionable food.

7. Surprise: The over-enthusiastic prankster who pops out of nowhere with a confetti cannon, always keeping everyone on their toes.

Emotions are complex psychological states that involve three distinct components: a subjective experience, a physiological response, and a behavioral or expressive response. They are responses to significant internal or external events and can affect our thoughts, behaviors, and actions.

Subjective Experience: This is the personal and internal feeling aspect of emotion, such as feeling happy, sad, angry, or fearful.

Physiological Response: This involves the body's reaction to emotions, such as changes in heart rate, respiration, hormone levels, and brain activity.

Behavioral Response: This includes the outward expression of emotions, such as facial expressions, body language, and actions.

Emotions are essential for survival as they help individuals respond to environmental challenges and opportunities.

Emotional Regulation

Emotional regulation is like having a quirky but effective team of bouncers at the club of your mind. Here's a humorous take:

1. **Joy-Bouncer**: The overly enthusiastic one who lets in all the happiness and excitement but occasionally needs to be reminded that not every moment is a dance party.

2. **Sadness-Security**: The compassionate bouncer who ensures that tears have their place but makes sure you don't end up crying over spilled milk (or coffee, or ice cream…).

3. **Anger-Manager:** The tough but fair bouncer who steps in to cool things down when tempers flare, preventing unnecessary bar fights over the last piece of cake.

4. **Fear-Guard:** The cautious protector who checks IDs (irrational fears) at the door, making sure only the legitimate concerns get in while the paranoia stays out.

5. **Disgust-Doorman**: The selective bouncer who helps you avoid bad decisions and questionable company, though sometimes he needs to chill out and let you enjoy that slightly burnt toast.

6. **Surprise-Sentinel**: The spontaneous one who loves to keep things exciting but is trained to prevent full-blown panic when surprises are less than pleasant.

7. **Love-Bouncer**: The sweet, gentle enforcer who makes sure love and affection get in but also knows when to close the door to avoid overattachment to your 97th houseplant.

8. **Jealousy-Watchdog**: The vigilant bouncer who keeps an eye on potential threats but learns to relax when someone else gets a promotion or the last slice of pizza.

Together, these bouncers help keep the emotional club of your mind running smoothly, making sure the right emotions come in at the right times and that the party never gets out of hand.

Emotional regulation refers to the ability to monitor, evaluate, and modify emotional reactions in order to achieve one's goals. It involves a range of processes and strategies that can influence which emotions one has, when one has them, and how one experiences and expresses these emotions.

Key aspects of emotional regulation include:

Awareness: Recognizing and understanding one's own emotions.

Acceptance: Being open to experiencing emotions without necessarily acting on them impulsively.

Control: The ability to manage and adjust emotional responses, often through techniques such as reappraisal, suppression, or problem-solving.

Adaptation: Using emotional responses constructively to navigate social interactions and achieve personal objectives.

Effective emotional regulation is crucial for mental health and well-being, helping individuals cope with stress, build healthy relationships, and maintain a balanced life.

Emotional Dysregulation and Narcissistic Personality Disorder (NPD)

Emotional dysregulation with a dash of narcissistic personality disorder is like having a wildly unpredictable reality TV show in your mind, starring a self-obsessed diva. Here's a humorous take:

1. **Drama King/Queen**: Every minor setback is an epic catastrophe. Didn't get enough likes on your selfie? Time to declare a national emergency!

2. **Mood Swings**: Your emotions have more plot twists than a soap opera. One minute you're on top of the world, the

next, you're convinced it's the end of days because someone didn't say "Good morning."

3. **Attention Hog**: Every conversation somehow circles back to you. "Sure, your trip to Paris sounds cool, but let me tell you about the time I took a perfect Instagram photo!"

4. **Validation Vampire**: You need constant praise to survive, like a vampire needs blood. No compliment is ever enough—did someone mention how amazing you look today? No? Unacceptable!

5. **Criticism Catastrophe**: Even the mildest criticism feels like a direct assault. "What do you mean I can't parallel park? Clearly, the car and the road are conspiring against my brilliance!"

6. **Blame Game**: Nothing is ever your fault. The universe is clearly out to get you. "I didn't forget the deadline; it's the calendar's fault for being so confusing!"

7. **Empathy Exit**: Empathy left the building long ago. Someone else's problem? Yawn. Let's get back to how fabulous you are.

8. **Emotional Rollercoaster**: Your emotions are like an unpredictable rollercoaster—exciting for about five minutes, then just nauseating. "I'm ecstatic! Now I'm furious! Now I'm sobbing! Wheee!"

Living with emotional dysregulation and narcissistic personality disorder is like starring in your own personal, never-ending drama where you're both the hero and the hapless victim, navigating a world that just doesn't appreciate your greatness quite enough.

Narcissistic Personality Disorder (NPD) is characterized by a persistent pattern of grandiosity, a need for admiration, and a lack of empathy. Emotional dysregulation, a significant component of NPD, exacerbates these traits, making emotional regulation a key area of concern for individuals with this disorder. Individuals with NPD often have substantial difficulties with emotional regulation. Emotional regulation refers to the processes by which individuals influence which emotions they have, when they have them, and how they experience and express these emotions. NPD patients struggle to manage their emotions effectively, leading to intense and often inappropriate emotional responses.

Emotional dysregulation is a significant challenge for individuals with Narcissistic Personality Disorder (NPD), arising from several core factors. Central personality traits such as grandiosity and entitlement often lead to extreme emotional responses when threats to self-image are perceived. This can result in disproportionate reactions to perceived slights or criticisms. Additionally, a lack of empathy makes it difficult for NPD patients to understand and respond appropriately to others' emotions, leading to maladaptive social interactions. Despite their outward confidence, many individuals with NPD have fragile self-esteem. This instability causes strong reactions to situations that challenge their self-worth. Developmental factors also play a role; NPD often develops from childhood experiences where emotional needs were either excessively indulged or harshly neglected, resulting in poor emotional regulation skills.

Clinical observations and empirical studies support the presence of emotional dysregulation in NPD. Patients with NPD often exhibit sudden and intense mood swings in response to minor events, frequent interpersonal conflicts due to an inability to manage emotions, and behavioral outbursts of rage or intense frustration when their self-image is challenged. For example, an individual might react explosively to a perceived minor insult, such as not being praised in a meeting, or might use emotions manipulatively, displaying charm or anger to achieve desired outcomes. They often exhibit a persistent need for validation, causing their mood to fluctuate dramatically based on external feedback.

Common signs and symptoms of emotional dysregulation in NPD patients include intense rage and hostility, often disproportionate to the situation, especially when their self-esteem is threatened. Depression and anxiety can be comorbid with NPD due to the chronic instability in self-worth.

These individuals also face difficulties in maintaining relationships due to manipulative behaviors and lack of empathy. They tend to have a low tolerance for criticism, often overreacting to any form of critique and viewing it as a personal attack.

Understanding these aspects of emotional dysregulation in NPD is crucial for developing effective therapeutic strategies. Cognitive-behavioral therapy (CBT) and dialectical behavior therapy (DBT) are often used to help individuals recognize and alter dysfunctional thought patterns and behaviors. In the Indian context, SEHT – Sunconscious Energy Healing Therapy works more effectively with individuals having NPD as also with their family members too. Techniques such as mindfulness and emotional regulation skills can be particularly effective in managing intense emotions and reducing maladaptive behaviors. Additionally, building empathy and improving interpersonal effectiveness are key goals in therapy to help NPD patients form healthier relationships.

In summary, emotional dysregulation in NPD is driven by core traits of grandiosity and entitlement, a lack of empathy, and fragile self-esteem, often stemming from developmental factors. Clinical manifestations include intense mood swings, interpersonal conflicts, and manipulative emotional behaviors. Effective therapeutic strategies focus on cognitive-behavioral approaches and skills training to improve emotional regulation, empathy, and interpersonal effectiveness, ultimately helping individuals with NPD lead more stable and fulfilling lives.

Emotional dysregulation is thus, a significant challenge for individuals with NPD. The inability to manage emotions effectively can lead to intense and inappropriate emotional responses, contributing to the interpersonal and psychological difficulties characteristic of the disorder. Understanding and addressing these emotional regulation issues is crucial for effective treatment and improving the quality of life for those with NPD.

Empathy and Narcissistic Personality Disorder (NPD)

Cognitive and Emotional Empathy

Cognitive empathy involves understanding another person's perspective, while emotional empathy entails sharing and responding to another's emotional state. Studies have shown that individuals with Narcissistic Personality Disorder (NPD) often have significant deficits in both cognitive and emotional empathy. For example, Ritter et al. (2011) found that individuals with NPD exhibited a pronounced lack of both types of empathy when compared to control groups, which suggests difficulties in both recognizing and connecting with the emotional experiences of others.

Variability in Empathic Functioning

Despite these general deficits, there is notable variability in empathic functioning among individuals with NPD. Baskin-Sommers et al. (2014) highlighted this variability through case studies, demonstrating that some individuals with NPD might exhibit situational or selective empathy. This selective empathy often serves their personal interests or helps maintain their grandiose self-image, and can be manipulative in nature. This suggests that while the capacity for empathy might exist, it is often employed in a self-serving manner rather than as a genuine emotional connection.

Understanding these nuances in empathic functioning is crucial for developing effective therapeutic approaches for NPD. Addressing the deficits in both cognitive and emotional empathy can help improve interpersonal relationships and reduce the manipulative behaviors often observed in individuals with NPD. Encouraging consistent, genuine empathic engagement rather than selective empathy may foster more meaningful and stable connections with others.

Emotional regulation for those suffering from NPD

Emotional regulation is crucial for individuals with Narcissistic Personality Disorder (NPD) to navigate their emotions effectively. Here are practical techniques to follow:

- **Mindfulness Meditation**: Spend a few minutes each day in quiet reflection. Focus on one's breathing and observe one's thoughts and feelings without judgment. With regular practice, one will become more aware of what triggers one's emotions and learn to respond calmly.
- **Positive Thinking**: Challenge negative thoughts by replacing them with positive and realistic ones. This shift in mindset can help one approach problems calmly, reducing feelings of being overwhelmed.
- **Relaxation Techniques**: During intense emotions, try deep breathing or muscle relaxation exercises. Label one's feelings and concentrate on positive experiences to better manage one's emotions.
- **Journaling**: Keep a daily journal to jot down one's thoughts and feelings. Reflect on these entries to identify patterns and triggers, gaining deeper insights into one's emotional landscape.
- **Physical Activity**: Engage in activities like walking or yoga to reduce stress and enhance one's overall mood.
- **Self-Reflection**: Regularly assess one's emotions and reactions to different situations. This self-awareness can empower you to make more informed choices.

- **Therapy**: Consider seeking therapy to explore and address underlying issues contributing to emotional dysregulation.
- **Healthy Relationships**: Surround one self with supportive individuals who understand and validate your experiences. Building a strong support system can provide stability during challenging times.
- **Self-Care**: Prioritize self-care by ensuring one gets enough sleep, eats well, and takes time to relax. These simple practices can significantly impact one's emotional well-being.
- **Avoid Isolation**: Resist the urge to isolate oneself, as it can exacerbate emotional dysregulation. Stay connected with others and seek support when needed.
- **Avoid Substance Abuse**: Refrain from using drugs or alcohol as coping mechanisms. These substances can worsen emotional control and lead to further complications.
- **Avoid Impulsive Reactions**: Take a moment to pause and consider your response before reacting emotionally. This deliberate approach can prevent impulsive behaviors and foster healthier interactions.
- **Challenge Negative Self-Talk**: Replace self-critical thoughts with positive affirmations. Cultivating self-compassion can help build resilience and improve self-esteem.

By incorporating these techniques into one's daily life and avoiding harmful behaviors, one can take proactive steps toward improving emotional regulation and overall well-being. Remember, progress takes time and patience, so be gentle with yourself throughout the journey

The Role of Friends and Family in Supporting Emotional Regulation for Individuals with NPD

Navigating emotional regulation for individuals with Narcissistic Personality Disorder (NPD) can be challenging, but the support of friends and family can significantly aid in this journey. Understanding the complexities of NPD and knowing how to respond effectively when emotional regulation issues arise are essential for loved ones. Here's what friends and family should understand, do, and action steps they can take to help individuals with NPD:

Understanding Emotional Regulation in NPD

1. **Complexity of Emotions**: Friends and family should recognize that individuals with NPD may struggle with regulating their emotions due to underlying insecurities and a fragile sense of self-worth.

2. **Impact on Relationships**: Emotional dysregulation in NPD can strain relationships and lead to conflicts. It's crucial for loved ones to approach these situations with empathy and patience.

What Friends and Family Should Do

1. **Provide Validation**: Offer validation and empathy to the individual with NPD, acknowledging their feelings without judgment. This creates a safe space for them to express themselves.

2. **Encourage Therapy**: Gently encourage the individual to seek therapy, such as Cognitive

Behavioral Therapy (CBT) or Dialectical Behavior Therapy (DBT), which can provide tools for managing emotions.

3. **Set Boundaries**: Establish clear and consistent boundaries to protect your own well-being while still offering support. This helps maintain healthy relationships.

Action Steps for Helping Individuals with NPD

1. **Practice Active Listening**: Listen attentively to the individual's concerns and validate their emotions without judgment.

2. **Encourage Self-Reflection**: Prompt the individual to reflect on their emotions and reactions, helping them develop greater self-awareness.

3. **Provide Emotional Support**: Offer reassurance and encouragement during difficult times, demonstrating empathy and understanding.

4. **Model Healthy Coping Mechanisms**: Lead by example by practicing healthy coping strategies, such as deep breathing or mindfulness, which the individual can emulate.

5. **Offer Gentle Guidance**: Provide gentle guidance when emotional dysregulation occurs, reminding the individual of coping techniques they've learned in therapy.

By understanding the challenges of emotional regulation in NPD, offering support, and taking proactive steps to help individuals with NPD manage their emotions, friends and family can play a crucial role in fostering emotional well-being and healthier relationships.

AI-Driven Emotion Recognition – Responsible AI

Emotions play a crucial role in human behavior and well-being, and effective regulation of emotions is essential for mental health. With the advancements in artificial intelligence (AI), various tools and applications have emerged to assist individuals in managing their emotions.

With the rapid advancements in technology, particularly in artificial intelligence (AI), there has been growing interest in developing AI-based tools to assist individuals in managing their emotions. These tools leverage machine learning algorithms and natural language processing techniques to provide personalized support and interventions for emotional regulation. The following segment aims to explore the current landscape of AI-based tools for emotional regulation, examining their development, functionalities, effectiveness, and ethical considerations.

Development of AI-Based Tools for Emotional Regulation:

AI-based tools for emotional regulation have been developed across various domains, including mental health care, education, and personal well-being. These tools utilize advanced AI techniques, such as sentiment analysis, affective computing, and virtual agents, to understand and respond to users' emotional states. For example, chatbots and virtual assistants equipped with emotional intelligence capabilities can engage users in conversations and provide empathetic responses based on their emotional cues .

Similarly, wearable devices integrated with AI algorithms can monitor users' physiological signals and provide real-time feedback to help regulate their emotions. Furthermore, mobile applications and web-based platforms use AI-driven interventions, such as cognitive-behavioral therapy (CBT) techniques and mindfulness exercises, to support users in managing stress, anxiety, and depression.

Functionalities of AI-Based Tools for Emotional Regulation:

AI-based tools for emotional regulation offer a wide range of functionalities to assist users in understanding, expressing, and regulating their emotions. These functionalities include:

1. **Emotion Recognition:** AI algorithms can analyze facial expressions, vocal intonations, and text inputs to recognize users' emotional states accurately.

2. **Personalized Interventions:** Based on users' emotional profiles and preferences, AI-powered tools can deliver personalized interventions, such as relaxation techniques, mood tracking, and self-reflection exercises.

3. **Feedback and Support:** AI chatbots and virtual agents provide users with empathetic responses, encouragement, and guidance to help them navigate emotional challenges.

4. **Skill-Building Activities:** AI-driven applications offer interactive activities and games to enhance users' emotional intelligence, empathy, and coping skills.

5. **Data Analytics:** AI tools analyze users' emotional data over time to identify patterns, trends, and potential risk factors for mental health issues.

Obstacles In Implementing Overcoming Narcissistic Challenges with AI For Regulating Emotions

Implementing AI to help overcome narcissistic challenges and regulate emotions involves a variety of obstacles, both technical and ethical:

1. **Complexity of Emotions and Personality Disorders**: Narcissism and emotional regulation involve complex psychological patterns that can vary significantly from one individual to another. AI models need vast amounts of data to understand and predict human emotions accurately, and this complexity increases with the nuanced nature of personality disorders like narcissism.

2. **Ethical Considerations**: Using AI to modify or regulate emotions, especially in individuals with narcissistic traits, raises significant ethical questions. There is a risk of manipulation and infringement on personal autonomy. Ensuring that these systems are used ethically and with the individual's consent is a major concern.

3. **Privacy Concerns**: Gathering the necessary personal data to train AI models on emotional states and personality traits raises privacy issues. Individuals may be reluctant to share sensitive information required for the AI to function effectively.

4. **Lack of Personalization:** AI systems might struggle to provide personalized care that takes into account the unique backgrounds, experiences, and needs of individuals.

Overcoming this requires AI models that can adapt and learn from each interaction, which is challenging to implement.

5. **Reliability and Accuracy:** The reliability of AI in interpreting human emotions and effectively responding to them is a critical concern. Misinterpretations can lead to inappropriate responses, potentially exacerbating the individual's emotional state or narcissistic tendencies.

6. **Dependency:** There's a risk of individuals becoming overly dependent on AI for emotional regulation, which could hinder their ability to develop intrinsic coping mechanisms and emotional resilience.

7. **Professional Oversight**: Integrating AI into therapeutic contexts for managing narcissism and emotional regulation requires careful oversight by professionals. Ensuring that AI applications are used as a complement to, rather than a replacement for, human therapists is essential.

8. **Regulatory Hurdles:** There are significant regulatory challenges to navigate, as the use of AI in mental health treatment is still an emerging field. Ensuring compliance with healthcare regulations and standards is essential for the safe and effective use of AI.

Addressing these obstacles requires a multidisciplinary approach, combining insights from psychology, computer science, ethics, and law to create AI systems that are effective, ethical, and respectful of individual autonomy and privacy.

Cultivating Mindfulness and Self-Compassion

Another effective approach for promoting emotional regulation is through the practice of mindfulness and self-compassion. Mindfulness involves paying attention to the present moment with openness, curiosity, and acceptance, while self-compassion involves treating oneself with kindness and understanding, especially in moments of difficulty or distress.

AI-powered mindfulness apps can guide individuals through meditation exercises, breathing techniques, and body scans designed to cultivate awareness of their thoughts, emotions, and physical sensations. By developing a greater sense of self-awareness and acceptance, individuals can learn to recognize and regulate their emotions more effectively, reducing the impact of narcissistic tendencies on their well-being and relationships.

Building Interpersonal Skills

In addition to regulating their own emotions, individuals with narcissistic tendencies may benefit from developing interpersonal skills such as empathy, active listening, and conflict resolution. AI-driven virtual reality simulations offer a safe and immersive environment for practicing these skills in realistic scenarios, allowing individuals to receive feedback and guidance in real-time.

By engaging in role-playing exercises and interactive scenarios, individuals can enhance their ability to empathize with others, communicate effectively, and resolve conflicts constructively. Over time, these skills can help individuals to build healthier and more fulfilling relationships, reducing the interpersonal difficulties often associated with narcissistic personality patterns.

Embracing AI for Emotional Regulation and NPD Management: A Call to Innovate

In recent years, the convergence of artificial intelligence (AI) and mental health has opened up new avenues for addressing the complex challenges associated with managing conditions like Narcissistic Personality Disorder (NPD). This fusion of technology and psychology offers a unique opportunity to revolutionize the way we approach emotional regulation and NPD management, with a primary focus on enhancing self-awareness and fostering personal growth. In this article, we delve into the significance of leveraging AI for emotional regulation and NPD management, highlighting opportunities for innovation and collaboration in this burgeoning field.

Why Focus on AI, Emotional Regulation, and NPD?

1. **Personalized Support:** AI-driven tools can provide tailored interventions to promote self-awareness and emotional regulation.
2. **Accessibility and Scalability:** AI-powered platforms can bridge gaps in mental health care by offering consistent support beyond traditional therapy sessions.
3. **Data-Driven Insights:** AI algorithms can uncover insights into NPD symptoms, triggers, and effective coping strategies, aiding researchers and clinicians in developing targeted interventions.

Opportunities for Innovation

- **Tech Startups:** Entrepreneurs can develop AI-driven virtual therapy platforms and mobile applications for self-reflection, offering on-demand support and personalized guidance.

- **Academic Research:** Researchers can explore the potential of AI-based emotion recognition technology to aid individuals with NPD in understanding their emotional states and developing coping strategies.

- **Government Initiatives:** Governments can support initiatives that promote the development and implementation of AI-driven tools for emotional regulation and NPD management, ensuring accessibility and affordability for all individuals in need.

- **Virtual Therapy Platforms:** Develop AI-driven virtual therapy platforms that offer on-demand support and interventions for individuals with NPD. These platforms can utilize natural language processing and sentiment analysis to provide empathetic responses and personalized guidance.

- **Emotion Recognition Technology:** Create AI-based tools that can accurately recognize and interpret facial expressions, vocal intonations, and text inputs associated with NPD symptoms. This technology can help individuals with NPD gain insight into their emotional states and develop effective coping strategies.

- **Mobile Applications for Self-Reflection:** Design mobile applications equipped with AI features for self-reflection and mood tracking. These applications can prompt users to journal their thoughts and feelings, analyze emotional patterns over time, and receive personalized feedback and suggestions for improvement.

- **Community Support Networks:** Establish online communities and support networks for individuals with NPD, facilitated by AI moderators. These platforms can foster peer support, share resources and coping strategies, and provide a safe space for individuals to connect and share their experiences.

The fusion of AI into emotional regulation and NPD management is a promising frontier in mental health. Through collaborative efforts among tech startups, academic research, and government initiatives, we can revolutionize the lives of those with NPD. By leveraging AI, we empower individuals to navigate emotions adeptly, fostering personal growth and self-discovery.

Ethical Considerations in AI-Based Tools for Emotional Regulation:

Despite the potential benefits of AI-based tools for emotional regulation, several ethical considerations need to be addressed to ensure their responsible development and use. These considerations include:

1. **Privacy and Data Security:** AI tools collect and analyze users' sensitive emotional data, raising concerns about privacy, confidentiality, and data security.

2. **Transparency and Accountability:** Users should be informed about the algorithms, data sources, and

decision-making processes used in AI tools to promote transparency and accountability.

3. **Bias and Fairness:** AI algorithms may exhibit biases in emotion recognition and intervention delivery, leading to unequal treatment and outcomes across diverse populations.

4. **Informed Consent:** Users should provide informed consent before using AI-based tools for emotional regulation, understanding the potential risks and benefits involved.

5. **Human Oversight:** Despite the autonomy of AI systems, human oversight is essential to ensure the ethical and responsible use of these tools, particularly in sensitive contexts such as mental health care.

Future Directions and Challenges:

The field of AI-based tools for emotional regulation is rapidly evolving, with ongoing advancements in technology and research. Future directions and challenges in this area include:

1. **Integration with Clinical Practice:** AI tools for emotional regulation need to be integrated into clinical practice and mental health care settings to reach a wider audience and maximize their impact.

2. **User-Centered Design:** Designing AI tools that are user-friendly, accessible, and culturally sensitive is essential to enhance user engagement and effectiveness.

3. **Long-Term Engagement:** Ensuring long-term user engagement and adherence to AI interventions for emotional regulation remains a significant challenge, requiring innovative strategies and incentives.

4. **Validation and Standardization:** There is a need for rigorous validation and standardization of AI tools for emotional regulation to ensure their reliability, validity, and effectiveness across diverse populations.

5. **Ethical Guidelines and Regulations:** Establishing ethical guidelines and regulations for the development and deployment of AI-based tools for emotional regulation is essential to protect users' rights, autonomy, and well-being.

AI-based tools hold great promise for assisting individuals in managing their emotions and promoting mental health and well-being. However, to realize their full potential, it is crucial to address ethical considerations, ensure their

Case study- The Journey of Mrs. Reema: A Tale of Redemption

Background

In the bustling city of Mumbai, amidst the chaotic streets and bustling markets, lived Mrs. Reema, a woman whose life appeared serene on the surface but harbored tumult within. At 42 years old, she exuded grace and charm, yet her inner turmoil threatened to engulf her entire existence. Married to Rahul, a kind-hearted man, and blessed with a daughter named Alisha, Mrs. Reema's life should have been a picture-perfect dream. However, her battle with

Narcissistic Personality Disorder (NPD) and emotional regulation issues cast a dark shadow over her family's happiness.

Signs and Symptoms

Mrs. Reema's struggles manifested in various ways, evident to those who knew her intimately:

1. **Grandiosity**: She often boasted about her achievements, seeking constant validation from others to mask her deep-seated insecurities.

2. **Lack of Empathy**: Her inability to empathize with Rahul's emotions led to frequent conflicts, leaving him emotionally drained and despondent.

3. **Impulsive Behavior**: Mrs. Reema's temper flared unpredictably, resulting in outbursts of rage and physical aggression towards Rahul.

4. **Manipulative Tendencies**: She manipulated situations to maintain control over her family

dynamics, oblivious to the damage wrought by her actions.

5. **Interpersonal Strife**: Her relationships were fraught with tension, characterized by a cycle of idealization followed by devaluation, leaving emotional scars on those closest to her.

Struggles and Realization

As her marriage teetered on the brink of collapse and Rahul spiraled into depression, Mrs. Reema found herself at a crossroads. Confronted with the wreckage of her family life, she begrudgingly sought therapy, hoping to salvage what remained of her fractured relationships. It was a journey fraught with resistance and denial, yet amidst the chaos, a glimmer of self-awareness emerged. Mrs. Reema began to unravel the tangled web of her psyche, peeling back layers of facade to confront the stark reality of her condition.

Treatment and Redemption

Therapy became her refuge, a sanctuary where she could confront her inner demons without fear of judgment. Through cognitive-behavioral techniques and dialectical behavior therapy, she learned to challenge her distorted beliefs and regulate her tumultuous emotions. It was a gradual process, marked by setbacks and triumphs, yet with each passing session, Mrs. Reema edged closer to redemption. She discovered the power of vulnerability, allowing herself to embrace her imperfections and cultivate empathy towards others.

Transformation and Impact

As Mrs. Reema embarked on her journey of self-discovery, a metamorphosis occurred. She shed the shackles of her NPD, emerging from the shadows of her past to embrace a newfound sense of authenticity. Her relationship with Rahul underwent a profound metamorphosis, blossoming into a union built on trust, understanding, and mutual respect. Alisha witnessed her mother's transformation with awe, inspired by her resilience and courage. Together, they forged a new path forward, guided by the beacon of hope that illuminated Mrs. Reema's once-darkened soul.

Mrs. Reema's journey is a testament to the indomitable human spirit, a tale of redemption forged in the crucible of adversity. Through perseverance and self-reflection, she transcended the confines of her disorder to reclaim her identity and rebuild her shattered relationships. Her story serves as a beacon of hope for those grappling with similar struggles, a reminder that even in the darkest of nights, the dawn of redemption awaits those brave enough to seek it.

In the chapters that follow, we will explore additional AI-driven techniques and strategies for addressing narcissistic challenges and fostering personal growth. By leveraging the power of technology and embracing new approaches to emotional regulation, individuals can overcome the limitations of narcissism and embark on a path of greater emotional well-being and fulfillment

Chapter 6:
Nurturing Empathy and Connection: AI's Role in Enhancing Interpersonal Relationships

In this chapter, we focus on how artificial intelligence can be utilized to nurture empathy and foster deeper connections in individuals displaying narcissistic personality patterns. Interpersonal relationships, often strained by the characteristics associated with narcissism, such as empathy deficits and a heightened focus on oneself, can benefit significantly from the targeted application of AI technologies. These tools offer innovative approaches to understanding and improving how individuals with narcissistic tendencies relate to others.

Characteristics of NPD and Relationship Impact

Narcissistic Personality Disorder (NPD) is a complex mental health condition marked by an exaggerated sense of self-importance, a constant need for admiration, and a lack of empathy for others. Individuals with NPD often display traits such as grandiosity, entitlement, and manipulative behavior. Recognizing these characteristics is essential for understanding NPD's effects on relationships.

Characteristics of NPD

1. **Grandiosity:** People with NPD exhibit an inflated sense of self-importance, seeking constant admiration and attention from others. They may exaggerate their achievements and dominate conversations.

2. **Need for Admiration:** NPD individuals crave excessive validation and may disregard others' feelings and contributions in pursuit of admiration.

3. **Lack of Empathy:** Empathy is notably absent in NPD, leading to difficulties in understanding or caring about others' emotions.

Impact on Relationships

1. **Dominance and Control:** NPD individuals strive for dominance in relationships, often resorting to manipulation tactics like gaslighting and guilt-tripping to maintain control.

2. **Emotional Rollercoaster:** Relationships with NPD individuals often oscillate between idealization and devaluation, with partners initially idolized and later criticized or emotionally abuse.

3. **Disregard for Boundaries:** NPD individuals may exploit their partners' emotions, seeking constant validation while neglecting their needs and autonomy.
4. **Fragile Self-Esteem:** Beneath their grandiose exterior lies fragile self-esteem, leading to a constant need for external validation and problematic relationship dynamics.

Red Flags and Early Warning Signs of Narcissistic Personality Disorder (NPD) in Relationships

1. Identifying Signs of NPD in Relationships

Charm

Narcissists often exhibit excessive charm and charisma at the beginning of relationships, making their partners feel special and valued. This phase, known as love bombing, can include grand gestures, constant attention, and lavish praise. This rapid progression in the relationship can be a red flag, as it is used to quickly gain the partner's trust and dependency.

Inconsistency

A hallmark of narcissistic behavior is inconsistency in words and actions. Narcissists may frequently change their opinions, exhibit unpredictable moods, or make promises they don't keep. This inconsistency can create confusion and insecurity in their partners, undermining their confidence and perception of the relationship.

Entitlement

Narcissists often display a sense of entitlement, believing they deserve special treatment and admiration. They may expect their partners to cater to their needs without reciprocating. This entitlement often manifests as a lack of empathy and consideration for the partner's feelings and needs.

2. Recognizing Patterns of Abuse

Gaslighting

Gaslighting is a form of psychological abuse where the narcissist manipulates their partner into doubting their reality, memories, or perceptions. This tactic is used to gain power and control, making the partner reliant on the narcissist's version of events. Signs of gaslighting include the narcissist denying past statements or actions, trivializing the partner's feelings, and insisting that the partner is overly sensitive or irrational.

Manipulation

Narcissists are skilled manipulators, often using tactics like guilt-tripping, blame-shifting, and playing the victim to maintain control over their partners. These behaviors can erode the partner's self-esteem and sense of autonomy. Recognizing these manipulative tactics is crucial for identifying and addressing the abusive dynamics in the relationship

Identifying early warning signs of NPD in relationships is critical. Look for excessive charm, inconsistency in behavior, and a sense of entitlement. Recognize patterns of gaslighting and manipulation as these are common abusive tactics used by narcissists to maintain control.

Prioritizing your wellbeing when you notice the red flags

If you recognize these red flags in your partner, it's essential to prioritize your well-being. Here's a set of actions you can consider taking.

1. **Trust your instincts:** Listen to your gut feelings and acknowledge any discomfort or unease you may be experiencing in the relationship.
2. **Set boundaries:** Clearly communicate your boundaries to your partner and assertively enforce them. It's important to establish healthy boundaries to protect yourself from manipulation or mistreatment.
3. **Seek support:** Reach out to friends, family members, or a therapist for support and guidance. Surrounding yourself with a supportive network can provide you with the strength and clarity you need to make difficult decisions.
4. **Plan your exit:** If you decide to end the relationship, plan your exit strategy carefully. Consider your safety and well-being, and seek assistance if necessary to ensure a smooth transition out of the relationship.
5. **Focus on self-care**: Prioritize self-care and healing as you navigate the aftermath of the relationship. Take time to process your emotions, engage in activities that bring you joy, and focus on rebuilding your confidence and self-esteem.

Ending a relationship with someone who exhibits narcissistic tendencies can be challenging, but prioritizing your well-being and setting healthy boundaries is essential for your emotional health and happiness.

Therapeutic Approaches in Interpersonal relationship management of NPD patients

Narcissistic Personality Disorder (NPD) makes it hard for people to maintain healthy relationships. However, therapy can help them develop better interpersonal skills and improve their relationships. Here are some effective therapies:

1. Mentalization-Based Treatment (MBT)

MBT teaches people with NPD to understand their own and others' thoughts and feelings. This helps them become more empathetic and better at handling emotions, which improves their interactions with others.

2. Cognitive-Behavioral Therapy (CBT)

CBT helps change negative thinking patterns and behaviors. For those with NPD, it focuses on reducing traits like entitlement and grandiosity, helping them respond better to criticism and build healthier relationships.

3. Schema Therapy

Schema Therapy looks at deeply rooted patterns and emotional needs. It helps people with NPD change these patterns, leading to more positive and less manipulative interactions with others.

4. Transference-Focused Psychotherapy (TFP)

TFP explores the relationship between the therapist and the patient. By understanding these interactions, patients can see how their internal conflicts affect their relationships and work towards resolving them.

5. Dialectical Behavior Therapy (DBT)

DBT teaches skills for managing emotions, tolerating distress, and improving relationships. For NPD patients, these skills help reduce manipulative behaviors and improve their interactions with others.

6. Psychodynamic Therapy

This long-term therapy helps patients understand the unconscious reasons behind their narcissistic behaviors. By bringing these reasons to light, they can develop healthier ways to relate to others and improve their relationships

SEHT (Subconscious Energy Healing Therapy) in Dealing with Interpersonal Relationship Management of NPD Patients

Subconscious Energy Healing Therapy (SEHT) is an innovative therapeutic modality that integrates traditional psychological practices with energy healing techniques to address the complexities of interpersonal relationship management, especially in the context of Narcissistic Personality Disorder (NPD). SEHT focuses on healing at the subconscious level, where deep-seated patterns and emotional wounds reside, thereby fostering healthier relationships and improving emotional well-being.

Understanding NPD and Interpersonal Relationships

NPD Characteristics:

- Grandiosity: Exaggerated sense of self-importance and superiority.

- Need for Admiration: Persistent craving for excessive attention and admiration.

- Lack of Empathy: Difficulty recognizing or considering the feelings of others.

- Manipulative Behaviors: Using others to achieve personal goals, often without regard for their well-being.

These traits often lead to challenging interpersonal relationships, characterized by manipulation, conflict, and emotional strain for both the NPD individual and their loved ones.

SEHT Principles and Techniques

1. Holistic Approach:

SEHT addresses the mind, body, and energy systems simultaneously, promoting comprehensive healing and well-being.

2. Subconscious Healing:

By accessing and healing the subconscious mind, SEHT targets the root causes of dysfunctional behaviors and emotional wounds.

3. Energy Balancing:

Techniques such as Reiki, chakra healing, and guided visualization are used to balance the body's energy, releasing blockages and promoting emotional stability.

Techniques for Managing Interpersonal Relationships with NPD Patients

1. Guided Imagery and Visualization:

Purpose:

- To help NPD individuals develop empathy and self-awareness.

- To provide loved ones with a mental space for processing emotions and building resilience.

Process:

- NPD patients are guided through visualizations that foster empathy, such as imagining themselves in others' shoes.

- Loved ones use visualization to create safe mental spaces where they can explore and release their emotions.

Example:

An NPD patient visualizes a scenario where they receive feedback from a loved one and respond with empathy and understanding, gradually internalizing this behavior.

2. **Chakra Healing and Energy Balancing**:

Purpose:

- To balance the energy centers affected by narcissistic traits, such as the solar plexus and heart chakras.

- To provide emotional relief and resilience for loved ones dealing with the emotional impact of NPD behaviors.

Process:

- NPD patients receive Reiki sessions focusing on balancing their energy centers, promoting emotional regulation and self-awareness.

- Loved ones receive chakra balancing to alleviate stress, anxiety, and emotional fatigue.

Example:

A regular Reiki session for an NPD patient targeting the heart chakra may help them open up to feelings of empathy and compassion, improving their interpersonal interactions.

3. **Emotional Release Techniques:**

Purpose:

- To help NPD individuals express and process suppressed emotions healthily.

- To support loved ones in releasing the emotional burdens caused by their interactions with NPD patients.

Process:

- Techniques such as journaling, expressive arts, and verbal expression are used to facilitate emotional release.

- Regular sessions focus on processing and integrating these emotions to promote healing.

Example:

An NPD patient engages in expressive art therapy to depict their inner emotional landscape, helping them recognize and address their suppressed emotions.

4. **Mindfulness and Meditation:**

Purpose:

- To cultivate self-awareness and emotional regulation in NPD individuals.

In conclusion, addressing the interpersonal challenges faced by individuals with Narcissistic Personality Disorder (NPD) requires a multifaceted therapeutic approach. Therapies such as Mentalization-Based Treatment, Cognitive-Behavioral Therapy, Schema Therapy, Transference-Focused

Psychotherapy, Dialectical Behavior Therapy, and Psychodynamic Therapy each offer unique strategies to improve empathy, emotional regulation, and self-awareness. By targeting the specific patterns and behaviors associated with NPD, these therapies help patients develop healthier relationships and enhance their overall social functioning. With consistent and empathetic treatment, individuals with NPD can make meaningful progress in their interpersonal interactions, leading to more fulfilling and stable relationships.

Navigating Relationships with NPD Individuals

Navigating relationships with individuals who have Narcissistic Personality Disorder (NPD) can be particularly challenging due to the distinct and often problematic characteristics associated with the disorder. People with NPD often exhibit traits such as grandiosity, a lack of empathy, a need for admiration, and a propensity for manipulative behaviors, which can strain and complicate interpersonal relationships. This article explores empirically sound strategies for managing these relationships, focusing on setting boundaries, developing support systems, employing effective communication, and resolving conflicts.

Setting Boundaries and Developing Support Systems

Setting Boundaries

Setting clear and firm boundaries is essential when dealing with individuals with NPD. Boundaries help protect your emotional well-being and prevent manipulative behaviors from causing harm. Here are some strategies for setting boundaries:

- **Identify Your Limits:** Understand what behaviors you can tolerate and what you cannot. This includes recognizing manipulative tactics like gaslighting, blame-shifting, and excessive criticism.
- **Communicate Clearly:** Clearly articulate your boundaries to the individual with NPD. Use direct and assertive language without being confrontational. For example, "I need to be spoken to respectfully, and I will not engage in conversations where I am being belittled."
- **Be Consistent:** Consistency is key to maintaining boundaries. Do not make exceptions, as this can lead to further manipulative behavior.
- **Enforce Consequences:** Be prepared to enforce consequences if boundaries are crossed. This could mean temporarily distancing yourself from the person or seeking external support.

Developing Support Systems

Having a strong support system is crucial for maintaining your mental health when dealing with someone with NPD. Support systems can include friends, family, and professional help:

- **Seek Social Support:** Surround yourself with people who understand your situation and can provide emotional support. Share your experiences with trusted friends or family members who can offer advice and encouragement.

- **Professional Help:** Therapy can be beneficial for both you and the individual with NPD. Therapists can provide coping strategies, validate your experiences, and help you develop healthier relationship dynamics. Cognitive-behavioral therapy (CBT) and dialectical behavior therapy (DBT) are effective therapeutic approaches for dealing with NPD traits.
- **Support Groups:** Joining support groups for people affected by NPD can provide a sense of community and shared experience. These groups offer a platform to discuss challenges and learn from others in similar situations.

Effective Communication and Conflict Resolution Strategies

Effective Communication

Communication with individuals with NPD requires a mindful and strategic approach to avoid escalating conflicts and misunderstandings. Here are some communication strategies:

- **Use "I" Statements:** Frame your concerns and needs using "I" statements to avoid sounding accusatory. For example, "I feel hurt when my opinions are dismissed" rather than "You always dismiss my opinions."
- **Stay Calm:** Keep your emotions in check during interactions. Showing anger or frustration can provoke defensive or aggressive responses from the person with NPD.

- **Focus on Specific Issues:** Address specific behaviors or incidents rather than making generalizations. This can help the person with NPD understand the impact of their actions without feeling attacked.
- **Avoid Criticism:** Criticism can trigger defensive reactions. Instead, focus on expressing your feelings and needs constructively.

Conflict Resolution Strategies

Resolving conflicts with individuals with NPD can be particularly challenging due to their difficulty in accepting fault and their tendency to manipulate situations. Effective conflict resolution strategies include:

- **Establish Common Ground:** Find areas of agreement to build a foundation for resolving conflicts. This can help reduce defensiveness and create a more cooperative environment.
- **Stay Solution-Focused:** Emphasize finding solutions rather than dwelling on the problem. Encourage collaborative problem-solving and compromise where possible.
- **Set Boundaries During Conflicts:** If the conflict escalates, be prepared to take a break and revisit the discussion later. This can prevent the situation from becoming more heated and unmanageable.
- **Seek Mediation:** In some cases, involving a neutral third party, such as a therapist or mediator, can help facilitate productive discussions and resolutions.

Practical Examples and Scenarios

To illustrate the strategies discussed, here are some practical examples and scenarios:

Scenario 1: Setting Boundaries with a Manipulative Partner

Imagine you are in a relationship with a partner who often uses manipulation to get their way. They might use guilt-tripping or play the victim to avoid taking responsibility for their actions. To set boundaries:

- **Identify Manipulative Behaviors:** Recognize when your partner is using manipulation, such as saying, "If you loved me, you would do this for me."
- **Communicate Boundaries:** Clearly state your boundaries by saying, "I need us to make decisions together without using guilt or manipulation."
- **Enforce Consequences:** If manipulation continues, enforce a consequence, such as taking a break from the conversation or seeking couples therapy.

Scenario 2: Effective Communication with a Narcissistic Family Member

Suppose you have a narcissistic family member who constantly criticizes and undermines you during family gatherings. To manage communication:

- **Use "I" Statements:** Express your feelings by saying, "I feel disrespected when my achievements are dismissed."

- **Stay Calm:** Keep your composure, even if they respond defensively. This helps you maintain control of the situation.

- **Focus on Specific Behaviors:** Address specific instances of criticism rather than labeling them as a critical person. For example, "When you said my promotion was not a big deal, it hurt my feelings."

Scenario 3: Conflict Resolution in the Workplace

Imagine you work with a colleague who has NPD traits and frequently takes credit for your work. To resolve conflicts:

- **Establish Common Ground:** Acknowledge their contributions to create a cooperative atmosphere. "I appreciate your input on this project."

- **Stay Solution-Focused:** Suggest solutions, such as setting clear roles and responsibilities for future projects to prevent credit-stealing.

- **Seek Mediation:** If the behavior continues, involve a supervisor or mediator to address the issue in a structured and neutral setting.

Navigating relationships with individuals with Narcissistic Personality Disorder requires a combination of setting clear boundaries, developing robust support systems, employing effective communication strategies, and utilizing conflict resolution techniques. By understanding the unique challenges posed by NPD and implementing these strategies, it is possible to manage and improve interpersonal relationships with individuals who exhibit narcissistic traits. Maintaining your mental well-being and seeking professional support when needed are crucial components of effectively handling these complex dynamics.

The Role of AI in Managing Relationships

Narcissistic Personality Disorder (NPD) presents significant challenges in interpersonal relationships due to traits like grandiosity, a lack of empathy, and manipulative behaviors. Traditional therapeutic approaches, while effective, can be augmented with artificial intelligence (AI) to provide continuous support and monitoring. This article explores how AI-driven mental health apps and virtual support groups, AI's role in monitoring behavioral patterns and providing emotional support, and specific examples of AI tools are transforming the management of relationships with NPD patients.

AI-Driven Mental Health Apps and Virtual Support Groups

AI-Driven Mental Health Apps

AI-driven mental health apps have emerged as valuable tools in managing NPD. These apps utilize advanced algorithms to offer personalized mental health support and resources. Some key benefits include:

- **Personalization:** AI algorithms can analyze user data to provide tailored recommendations and coping strategies. For instance, apps like Woebot and Youper use AI to engage users in therapeutic conversations, helping them manage stress, anxiety, and other emotional challenges.

- **Accessibility:** These apps are available 24/7, providing support whenever needed. This is

particularly beneficial for individuals in crisis or those needing immediate assistance.
- **Anonymity:** Users may feel more comfortable discussing sensitive issues with an AI than with a human therapist, reducing the stigma associated with seeking help.

Virtual Support Groups

Virtual support groups powered by AI offer a platform for individuals dealing with NPD to connect with others facing similar challenges. Key features include:

- **Facilitation of Communication:** AI can moderate discussions, ensuring they remain supportive and constructive. This helps maintain a safe space for participants.
- **Resource Sharing:** AI can curate and share relevant resources based on the group's discussions, such as articles, videos, and coping strategies.
- **Emotional Support:** AI can provide real-time emotional support through chatbots, helping users feel heard and validated.

For example, the app Talkspace offers AI-assisted therapy sessions where users can communicate with licensed therapists through text, audio, or video, providing a flexible and accessible way to seek professional help.

Using AI to Monitor Behavioral Patterns and Provide Emotional Support

Monitoring Behavioral Patterns

AI's ability to analyze large datasets can be leveraged to monitor the behavioral patterns of individuals with NPD. This involves:

- **Behavioral Analysis:** AI can track changes in behavior and mood through various inputs such as social media activity, wearable device data, and self-reported metrics. This continuous monitoring can help identify triggers and patterns associated with NPD behaviors.

- **Predictive Analytics:** By analyzing historical data, AI can predict potential crises or emotional breakdowns, enabling preemptive intervention. For instance, an AI system might detect a pattern of increased irritability and decreased social interaction, indicating a potential escalation in narcissistic behavior.

- **Feedback Loop:** AI can provide real-time feedback to both patients and therapists, facilitating more informed therapeutic interventions. This continuous loop helps in adjusting treatment plans based on the evolving needs of the patient.

Providing Emotional Support

AI can offer emotional support by simulating human-like interactions and empathy. This includes:

- **Chatbots:** AI-powered chatbots like Woebot can engage users in conversations designed to offer emotional support and cognitive-behavioral therapy (CBT) techniques. These interactions can help users manage stress, anxiety, and other emotional challenges.

- **Sentiment Analysis:** AI can analyze the emotional tone of user communications to offer appropriate responses and support. This helps in providing timely and relevant emotional assistance.
- **Personalized Interventions:** Based on the monitored data, AI can suggest personalized interventions such as mindfulness exercises, relaxation techniques, and coping strategies.

AI is playing a transformative role in managing relationships with individuals with Narcissistic Personality Disorder. By leveraging AI-driven mental health apps and virtual support groups, monitoring behavioral patterns, and providing emotional support, individuals can better navigate the complexities of these relationships. Specific AI tools like Woebot, Youper, Talkspace, and Replika offer innovative solutions that enhance traditional therapeutic approaches, providing continuous and personalized support. As AI technology continues to advance, its potential to improve mental health care and support for those dealing with NPD will only grow, offering new hope and resources for managing these challenging relationships.

Harnessing AI for Interpersonal Relationship Enhancement and NPD Management: A Call to Innovate

The integration of artificial intelligence (AI) with interpersonal relationships and Narcissistic Personality

Disorder (NPD) management offers a groundbreaking opportunity to revolutionize human interactions and mental health care. Entrepreneurs, researchers, and government initiatives are urged to champion the integration of AI into these domains, driving significant advancements in personal growth and well-being.

Why Focus on AI, Interpersonal Relationships, and NPD?

1. **Understanding and Empathy:** AI tools can analyze communication nuances, tone, and body language, fostering deeper understanding and empathy.
2. **Conflict Resolution:** AI algorithms can detect conflict triggers and propose constructive resolutions, promoting healthier communication and relationships,
3. **Self-Awareness:** AI insights can aid individuals with NPD in recognizing their behavior's impact on others, fostering self-awareness and personal growth .

Opportunities for Innovation

1. **Tech Startups:** Tech startups can lead the development of AI-driven virtual coaches and relationship health monitoring apps, catering to the growing demand for personalized mental health solutions.
2. **Academic Research:** Academic research can explore innovative uses of AI, such as emotion recognition technology, to enhance interpersonal

interactions and support individuals with NPD on their journey towards self-improvement.

3. **Government Initiatives:** Government initiatives can support AI-driven projects in mental health care, providing funding and resources to accelerate innovation and improve access to cutting-edge technologies for all individuals.

4. **Collaborative Efforts:** Collaborations between tech startups, academic institutions, and government agencies can foster interdisciplinary research and development, leading to holistic solutions that address the diverse needs of individuals affected by NPD and interpersonal challenges.

5. **Virtual Relationship Coaches:** AI-driven virtual coaches offer personalized guidance for enhancing communication skills and managing NPD traits.

6. **Emotion Recognition Technology:** AI-based tools recognize emotional cues in real-time, facilitating more empathetic interactions.

7. **Relationship Health Monitoring Apps:** Mobile apps equipped with AI track relationship dynamics, provide feedback, and suggest improvement strategies.

8. **Community Support Networks:** Online communities moderated by AI offer peer support, share resources, and provide guidance for individuals navigating interpersonal relationships and NPD.

In conclusion, AI's integration holds great promise for fostering healthier connections and supporting personal growth, marking a significant step forward in mental well-being.

Case Study: Love, Control, and Resilience: Reena's Journey to Self-Empowerment

Reena's life took an unexpected turn at the age of 34. A vibrant and capable businesswoman, she married a divorcee, believing in the promise of a loving partnership and a new family. From the very beginning, Reena showcased her compliant nature, easily adapting to her new husband's family dynamics. Her role quickly evolved into that of a dedicated caregiver, primarily tending to her husband's ailing mother, whose needs were both demanding and constant. Reena's days were filled with the routines of caregiving, including the more intimate tasks like changing diapers, and she performed these duties with unwavering dedication.

Despite her capabilities, Reena found herself economically dependent. Her husband controlled the family finances, leaving her without an independent bank account or financial autonomy. This control extended far beyond money. Reena's husband systematically isolated her from her own family and friends, cutting her off from the very networks that could have provided support and solace. Every outing required his permission, effectively putting Reena under house arrest in her own home.

The emotional toll was immense. Her husband's words were laced with criticism and judgment, chipping away at Reena's self-esteem. Every aspect of her life was scrutinized, and the constant belittlement made her question her own worth. This emotional manipulation created a shadow over Reena's vibrant personality, making her feel small and insignificant.

The financial dependence Reena endured further exacerbated the power imbalance in their relationship. Without access to her own financial resources, she had little choice but to comply with her husband's dictates. This economic stranglehold meant that leaving or asserting any independence felt impossible. Over time, the stress of her situation began to manifest in her health. Reena, already managing diabetes, found her condition worsening under the strain of constant emotional abuse and financial control.

A Path to Healing

Reena finally decided to seek help through psychotherapy, starting with Cognitive Behavioral Therapy (CBT). In her initial sessions, Reena worked with her therapist to identify and challenge the negative thought patterns that had taken root due to years of narcissistic abuse. Her therapist helped her recognize that the constant criticism and belittlement were not reflections of her worth but tactics of control used by her husband. Through CBT, Reena began to reframe these thoughts, slowly rebuilding her self-esteem and sense of self-worth.

As Reena progressed, her therapy sessions focused on developing practical strategies to regain control over her life. She learned assertiveness techniques, which empowered her to set boundaries with her husband. Role-playing exercises during sessions allowed Reena to practice these new skills in a safe environment, building her confidence to apply them in real life.

In addition to CBT, Reena's therapist introduced elements of trauma-focused therapy to address the deep-seated emotional scars left by the abuse. Through guided imagery and mindfulness exercises, Reena learned to process her trauma, reducing the anxiety and depression that had plagued her.

Over time, Reena's health began to improve. She found the strength to reconnect with her family and friends, rebuilding the support network that had been severed. Her improved mental health positively impacted her diabetes management, as she adopted healthier coping mechanisms and stress reduction techniques.

Role that AI could play:

In this digital age, Reena's path to self-empowerment could be significantly aided by AI-powered tools. These tools could play a pivotal role in recognizing patterns, offering support, and providing resources that might otherwise be inaccessible.

1. **Pattern Recognition**: AI algorithms could analyze her husband's behavior, identifying recurring patterns of control, manipulation, and isolation. This could help Reena understand the dynamics of her relationship and recognize the harmful impact it was having on her well-being.

2. **Emotional Support**: AI-powered chatbots or virtual assistants could offer Reena a supportive and non-judgmental space to express her emotions. These tools could provide her with coping strategies, validation, and resources for seeking help, making her feel less alone in her struggle.

3. **Education and Resources**: AI platforms could educate Reena about emotional abuse, healthy relationship dynamics, and financial empowerment. Increasing her knowledge could help her understand her options and make informed decisions about her future.
4. **Safety Planning**: AI-driven safety planning tools could assist Reena in developing a personalized plan to protect herself in dangerous situations. These tools could help her assess the level of risk in her relationship, identify warning signs of escalation, and create a step-by-step plan for seeking help and accessing resources.

By leveraging these AI-powered tools and resources, Reena could gain insight into her situation, access support and guidance, and take steps towards reclaiming her autonomy, safety, and well-being.

Reena's journey is a testament to the strength and resilience that can emerge from even the most challenging situations. It highlights the importance of recognizing and addressing the subtle and overt forms of control that can undermine an individual's sense of self. With the right support and tools, Reena, and others in similar situations, can find a path to empowerment and freedom.

Chapter 7:
Nurturing Empathy and Connection: AI's Role in Enhancing Interpersonal Relationships-

Artificial Intelligence (AI) plays a pivotal role in nurturing empathy and enhancing interpersonal relationships by facilitating deeper understanding and communication between individuals. AI-driven tools, such as emotion recognition software and natural language processing, enable more accurate interpretation of emotional cues and language nuances, fostering greater empathy and connection. These technologies can analyze speech patterns, facial expressions, and text to provide insights into the emotional states of individuals, helping users respond more compassionately and appropriately.

Additionally, AI can offer personalized recommendations for improving communication strategies, conflict resolution, and emotional support, thereby enhancing the quality of interactions. By bridging gaps in emotional understanding and providing tailored guidance, AI contributes to more meaningful and empathetic relationships, both in personal and professional settings.

Are NPD Patients Monsters? Shifting Perspectives: From Demonization to Understanding

Historically, individuals with Narcissistic Personality Disorder (NPD) have been labeled as inherently malicious or evil, reinforcing negative stereotypes. NPD has long been viewed through a lens of stigmatization and demonization, often leading to misunderstandings about those who suffer from it.

NPD is characterized by pervasive patterns of grandiosity, a need for admiration, and a lack of empathy (American Psychiatric Association, 2013). Despite the clinical definition, public perception often paints individuals with NPD as "monsters," a term that carries significant stigma and misunderstanding. This article aims to dismantle this myth by examining the diagnostic criteria, underlying psychological and social factors, and potential treatment avenues for NPD, thereby providing a more comprehensive understanding of the disorder.

The portrayal of individuals with NPD as "monsters" is largely fueled by media and popular culture, which often emphasize the most extreme and negative aspects of the disorder. However, empirical studies indicate that while NPD can result in harmful behaviors, individuals with this disorder are not inherently evil or malicious. Instead, their actions are often driven by deep-seated insecurities and maladaptive coping mechanisms to maintain self-esteem (Campbell & Miller, 2011).

Challenging the Monster Narrative

1. **Understanding the Complexity of NPD**

NPD is a multifaceted disorder that encompasses a range of symptoms and behaviors. While individuals with NPD may exhibit manipulative or narcissistic traits, they are not inherently monsters. Instead, they are individuals struggling with underlying psychological vulnerabilities and maladaptive coping mechanisms (Miller et al., 2010). Recognizing the complexity of NPD is essential for fostering empathy and understanding towards patients.

2. **Addressing Stigma and Misconceptions**

The monster narrative surrounding NPD perpetuates stigma and deters individuals from seeking help. By challenging misconceptions and promoting accurate information about NPD, we can reduce stigma and encourage individuals to access appropriate treatment and support (Pincus & Lukowitsky, 2010). Education and awareness campaigns play a crucial role in debunking myths and fostering empathy towards individuals with NPD.

A Holistic Approach to Treatment

1. **Fostering Empathy and Compassion**

Empathy is a cornerstone of effective treatment for NPD. By fostering empathy towards individuals with NPD, healthcare professionals can establish trust and rapport, facilitating therapeutic progress (Gabbard, 2014). Empathetic listening and validation empower individuals with NPD to engage in the therapeutic process.

2. **Setting Boundaries and Limits**

Setting boundaries is essential when working with individuals with NPD. Boundaries protect caregivers from emotional manipulation and burnout while promoting accountability and responsibility for patients (Goulston, 2012). Clear and consistent boundaries help maintain a therapeutic alliance while ensuring the safety and well-being of both parties.

3. **Promoting Self-Care Practices**

Caring for individuals with NPD can be emotionally taxing, necessitating self-care practices for caregivers. Engaging in activities that promote relaxation, stress relief, and emotional regulation is essential for maintaining psychological and physical well-being (Goulston, 2012). Self-care practices such as mindfulness, exercise, and social support networks help caregivers navigate the challenges of supporting individuals with NPD.

Treating individuals with NPD as monsters perpetuates stigma and hinders effective treatment. By adopting a holistic approach that prioritizes empathy, boundaries, and self-care, we can support individuals with NPD while safeguarding our own psychological and physical well-being. Challenging the monster narrative and fostering empathy towards individuals with NPD are essential steps in promoting compassionate and effective care for all.

The characterization of individuals with NPD as "monsters" is a harmful and inaccurate representation that overlooks the complexity and humanity of those affected by the disorder. By understanding the diagnostic criteria, underlying psychological and social factors, and available treatment options, it becomes evident that NPD is a multifaceted mental health condition that warrants empathy and evidence-based intervention. Continued research and public education are essential to destigmatize NPD and promote effective treatment strategies, ultimately fostering a more compassionate and informed perspective on this challenging disorder.

Can people with NPD change?

Change in individuals with NPD is challenging due to the deep-seated nature of their personality traits. The disorder is characterized by an exaggerated sense of self-importance and a profound need for attention and admiration.

However, there is some evidence that with long-term, consistent therapeutic intervention, individuals with NPD can exhibit changes. The capacity for change in individuals with Narcissistic Personality Disorder (NPD) is a complex and nuanced issue. While change is possible, it typically requires significant self-awareness, motivation, and sustained effort. Here are some key factors to consider when evaluating the potential for change in individuals with NPD:

1. **Motivation for Change**: Individuals with NPD may be motivated to change if they recognize the negative impact of their behavior on themselves and others, and if they desire to improve their relationships and overall well-being. However, motivation for change may be hindered by the individual's resistance to acknowledging personal flaws or vulnerability, which are central aspects of NPD.

2. **Therapeutic Intervention**: Psychotherapy, particularly modalities such as psychodynamic therapy or cognitive-behavioral therapy, can be effective in treating NPD by addressing maladaptive patterns of thinking and behavior. Therapy provides a safe and supportive environment for individuals with NPD to explore their emotions, motivations, and interpersonal dynamics, leading to greater self-awareness and insight.

3. **Development of Empathy**: Empathy, the ability to understand and share the feelings of others, is often impaired in individuals with NPD. However, with therapy and introspection, individuals with NPD can develop greater empathy by learning to recognize and validate the experiences of others, which can lead to more meaningful and authentic connections with others.

4. **Commitment to Personal Growth**: Change in individuals with NPD requires a commitment to personal growth and self-improvement. This may involve challenging long-held beliefs and behaviors, confronting uncomfortable emotions, and actively practicing new ways of relating to oneself and others.

5. **Supportive Environment**: A supportive environment, including understanding and compassionate relationships with family, friends, and mental health professionals, can facilitate the process of change for individuals with NPD. Supportive relationships provide validation, encouragement, and accountability, which are essential for sustaining progress and overcoming setbacks.

It's important to note that change in individuals with NPD is not guaranteed and may occur gradually over time. Additionally, the degree of change may vary depending on the individual's level of insight, motivation, and willingness to engage in the therapeutic process. While change is possible, it requires patience, persistence, and a holistic approach that addresses the underlying factors contributing to NPD.

Do Patients with NPD Feel Guilt and Regret?

Navigating the emotional landscape of a patient with Narcissistic Personality Disorder (NPD) can be like trying to find humility at a superhero convention. Do patients with NPD feel guilt and regret? Well, asking them to feel genuine remorse is akin to asking a cat to fetch your slippers – theoretically possible but highly unlikely. They might exhibit a performance of guilt or regret if it serves their grandiose narrative or gets them the admiration they crave, but true introspection is about as rare as a unicorn in a corporate boardroom. So, while they might occasionally throw out a "Sorry" like confetti at a parade, don't hold your breath waiting for heartfelt apologies or deep self-reflection!

Yes, Individuals with Narcissistic Personality Disorder (NPD) can experience pain and regret, although their experience of these emotions may differ from that of individuals without the disorder. Here's how pain and regret may manifest in individuals with NPD:

1. **Pain:** While individuals with NPD often present a facade of grandiosity and invulnerability, they are not immune to emotional pain. Underneath their outward bravado, individuals with NPD may experience feelings of insecurity, shame, and inadequacy. However, they may be highly adept at masking or denying these feelings, as acknowledging vulnerability goes against their self-image of perfection and superiority.

2. **Regret**: Individuals with NPD may struggle with experiencing genuine regret for their actions, particularly if doing so requires acknowledging fault or taking responsibility for their behavior. Instead, their expressions of regret may be superficial or insincere, serving to manipulate or control others rather than genuinely atoning for their actions. Additionally, individuals with NPD may have difficulty empathizing with the perspectives of others, making it challenging for them to understand the impact of their actions on those around them.

It's important to note that the experience of pain and regret in individuals with NPD may vary depending on the individual and the context of their relationships and experiences. While some individuals with NPD may exhibit limited capacity for experiencing and expressing these emotions, others may demonstrate greater insight and self-awareness, allowing them to acknowledge and grapple with their own vulnerabilities and shortcomings.

How can you empathise with someone who causes you pain?

Empathizing with someone who causes you pain is like trying to find the silver lining in a raincloud that just ruined your favorite outdoor event. It's a bit like hugging a cactus—you know it's theoretically possible, but you're bound to get poked. Picture yourself saying, "I totally get why you decided to spill coffee on my brand-new white shirt. You must have been deeply stressed and needed a caffeine-infused outlet for your frustration. I completely understand." Sure, it might feel a bit like trying to high-five a shark, but hey, at least you're giving it a shot, right? Finding empathy in such situations is like searching for a needle in a haystack while wearing mittens, but who knows, you might just discover that needle has a soft side too.

Yes, Empathizing with someone who has Narcissistic Personality Disorder (NPD) and is causing you pain can be particularly challenging due to the nature of the disorder. However, it is still possible to cultivate empathy while also protecting your own well-being. Here's how you can empathize with an individual with NPD:

- **Understand the Disorder**: Educate yourself about Narcissistic Personality Disorder to gain insight into the behaviors and thought patterns associated with the condition. Recognize that individuals with NPD often have deep-seated insecurities and fears of abandonment, which may manifest as defensive or hurtful behavior towards others.
- **Recognize Their Pain**: Acknowledge that individuals with NPD may be experiencing internal turmoil and emotional distress, even if they do not openly express it. Their grandiose facade and manipulative behaviors may be defense mechanisms to protect themselves from feelings of vulnerability and inadequacy.
- **Separate the Person from the Disorder**: Remember that the individual's hurtful actions are a result of their NPD and are not a reflection of their true self. Differentiate between the disorder and the person's inherent worth and humanity. By recognizing their struggles as

symptoms of NPD, you can empathize with their pain while still holding them accountable for their behavior.
- **Practice Boundaries**: Set clear and assertive boundaries to protect yourself from further harm while still empathizing with the individual. Communicate your needs and limits calmly and firmly, and enforce consequences if necessary. Boundaries are essential for maintaining your emotional and psychological well-being in relationships with individuals with NPD.
- **Validate Their Feelings**: Validate the individual's emotions and experiences, even if you disagree with their actions or behaviors. Let them know that you understand they may be struggling and that their feelings are valid. Validation can help foster a sense of connection and understanding, which may facilitate healthier communication and interactions.
- **Seek Support**: Reach out to trusted friends, family members, or mental health professionals for support and guidance. Discussing your experiences with others can provide validation, perspective, and coping strategies for dealing with the challenges of empathizing with someone with NPD.

Empathizing with someone who has NPD requires understanding, patience, and self-awareness. By acknowledging the individual's struggles, setting boundaries, and seeking support, you can cultivate empathy while also prioritizing your own well-being in the relationship.

Differentiating empathy from forgiveness

When dealing with an individual with Narcissistic Personality Disorder (NPD), it is crucial to differentiate between empathy and forgiveness. Understanding these concepts can help friends and family members manage their relationships with the NPD individual more effectively, ensuring their own well-being while providing appropriate support.

Empathy:

1. **Understanding Without Enabling**: Empathy involves understanding the emotional and psychological struggles that an NPD individual faces. Recognizing that their behaviors often stem from deep-seated insecurities and past traumas can foster a compassionate approach without condoning harmful actions.

2. **Maintaining Boundaries**: Practicing empathy means acknowledging the NPD individual's feelings while setting clear boundaries to protect oneself from manipulation and abuse. Empathy does not mean tolerating or excusing harmful behavior but rather approaching the situation with compassion.

3. **Effective Communication**: Empathy can lead to more productive and less confrontational communication. By showing understanding, family members and friends can potentially reduce conflicts and foster a more cooperative relationship.

Forgiveness:

1. **Letting Go of Resentment**: Forgiveness involves letting go of resentment and anger towards the NPD individual. This can be beneficial for one's own mental health, reducing stress and promoting emotional healing.

2. **Not a Reconciliation Requirement**: Forgiving someone with NPD does not necessarily mean reconciling with them or continuing the relationship. It is about freeing oneself from negative emotions and not holding on to past grievances.

3. **Personal Peace**: Forgiveness is more about achieving personal peace rather than changing the NPD individual. It is an internal process that can help one move forward without the burden of past hurts .

Differentiating Empathy and Forgiveness

- **Purpose**: Empathy focuses on understanding the NPD individual's condition and maintaining a compassionate perspective, while forgiveness is about letting go of negative emotions for personal well-being.

- **Boundaries**: Empathy requires setting firm boundaries to prevent enabling harmful behavior, whereas forgiveness is about internal emotional release and does not necessitate ongoing interaction.

- **Outcome**: Empathy aims to improve communication and manage interactions constructively, whereas forgiveness seeks to heal personal emotional wounds, irrespective of the future of the relationship.

Balancing empathy and forgiveness is essential for friends and family members dealing with an NPD individual. Empathy can foster understanding and effective communication, while forgiveness can help in personal emotional healing. However, it is important to maintain boundaries and prioritize one's own well-being to navigate these complex relationships successfully.

Understanding Guilt and Self-Blame in Non-NPD Individuals with NPD Loved Ones

Understanding guilt and self-blame in non-NPD individuals who have loved ones with NPD is like trying to solve a Rubik's Cube while riding a unicycle – it's tricky, and you're likely to fall a few times. These empathetic souls often find themselves caught in a web of "What did I do wrong?" as their narcissistic loved ones deftly shift blame with the finesse of a magician pulling a rabbit out of a hat. It's like being in a perpetual game of emotional dodgeball, where you're always the target, and the rules keep changing. Despite their best efforts to be supportive, they end up feeling like the villain in a soap opera plot twist. But remember, sometimes the only thing they did wrong was caring too much about someone who thinks they're the center of the universe – and no, the universe doesn't come with a user manual for that!

Yes,Dealing with a loved one who has Narcissistic Personality Disorder (NPD) can be emotionally challenging. Friends, family members, and romantic partners often experience intense feelings of guilt and self-blame. Understanding these emotions and learning to manage them is crucial for maintaining mental health and well-being.

Sources of Guilt and Self-Blame

1. **Manipulation and Gaslighting:** Individuals with NPD often engage in manipulative behaviors, such as gaslighting, which can make others question their own reality and feel responsible for the narcissist's negative behavior. This constant self-doubt can lead to pervasive guilt.

2. **Failed Attempts to Help**: Non-NPD individuals often feel guilty when their efforts to help or change the NPD person's behavior fail. They might believe they didn't try hard enough or weren't supportive enough.

3. **Blaming Themselves for Conflict:** Because NPD individuals tend to project blame onto others, friends and family members might internalize this blame, believing they are at fault for conflicts and issues within the relationship.

Psychological Impact

1. **Lowered Self-Esteem:** Constant criticism and blame from an NPD individual can erode the self-esteem of those around them, leading to a cycle of self-blame and feelings of inadequacy.

2. **Chronic Stress and Anxiety**: The unpredictable and often hostile behavior of someone with NPD can create a stressful environment, leading to chronic

anxiety and feelings of helplessness in non-NPD individuals.

3. **Depression:** Prolonged exposure to manipulation and emotional abuse can contribute to depression. Non-NPD individuals may feel trapped and hopeless, believing they are to blame for their loved one's behavior and their own resulting misery.

Managing Guilt and Self-Blame

1. **Education and Awareness**: Learning about NPD can help non-NPD individuals understand that the narcissist's behavior is not their fault. This knowledge can mitigate feelings of guilt and self-blame.

2. **Setting Boundaries**: Establishing and maintaining firm boundaries is essential. This helps protect one's own mental health and prevents further emotional manipulation.

3. **Seeking Support**: Therapy or support groups can provide a safe space to express feelings and receive validation. Professional guidance can help individuals navigate their complex emotions and develop coping strategies.

4. **Self-Compassion**: Practicing self-compassion involves treating oneself with kindness and understanding, recognizing that everyone makes mistakes and that one's worth is not determined by the behavior of others.

Dealing with a loved one who has NPD is fraught with emotional challenges, particularly feelings of guilt and self-blame. By educating themselves, setting boundaries, seeking support, and practicing self-compassion, non-NPD individuals can better manage these emotions and protect their own mental health. Understanding that the narcissist's behavior is not their fault is a critical step in mitigating these detrimental feelings and fostering a healthier emotional state.

Ensuring the Psychological Well-being of Children with Narcissistic Parents

Ensuring the psychological well-being of children with narcissistic parents involves creating a safe and supportive environment that counterbalances the potential emotional turbulence at home. It's crucial to provide these children with consistent love, validation, and understanding, helping them to develop a healthy sense of self-worth independent of their parent's influence. Encouraging open communication, allowing them to express their feelings and experiences without fear of judgment, can foster emotional resilience.

Providing access to therapy or counseling can be instrumental in helping them process their experiences and build coping strategies. Involvement in supportive social networks, such as school activities and community groups, can also offer positive reinforcement and a sense of belonging. By promoting these protective factors, caregivers and educators can help mitigate the effects of narcissistic parenting and support the child's emotional and psychological development.

Children in families with one or both parents suffering from Narcissistic Personality Disorder (NPD) face significant psychological and emotional challenges.

Strategies for Ensuring Psychological Well-being for Children with Narcissistic Parents

1. Therapeutic Interventions

a. Engage in Individual Therapy

- Seek cognitive-behavioral therapy (CBT) to develop healthy coping mechanisms, challenge distorted thinking, and build self-esteem. This provides a safe space for children to express emotions and process experiences.

b. Participate in Family Therapy

- If possible, involve the narcissistic parent in family therapy to improve communication, set healthy boundaries, and develop supportive interactions.

c. Join Group Therapy and Support Groups

- Connect with peers in group therapy or support groups to find validation, reduce isolation, and develop social skills.

2. Educational Support

a. Utilize School Counseling Services

- Work with school counselors for emotional support, identifying signs of distress, and receiving academic accommodations to succeed despite a challenging home environment.

b. Promote Teacher Training and Awareness

- Encourage teachers to recognize signs of emotional distress and understand NPD's impact on children, fostering a nurturing and supportive classroom environment.

3. Building a Supportive Environment

a. Leverage Extended Family and Friends

- Build a strong support network with extended family and friends for emotional support, stability, and positive role models. Regular interactions with supportive adults can buffer the negative impact of the narcissistic parent.

b. Engage with Community and Religious Organizations

- Participate in community and religious organizations that offer counseling services, support groups, and activities promoting social engagement and emotional well-being.

4. Legal and Protective Measures

a. Understand Legal Rights

- Seek legal counsel to understand protections against emotional and psychological abuse. In severe cases, consider legal intervention to ensure the child's safety and well-being.

b. Involve Child Protective Services

- If the child's well-being is at serious risk, contact child protective services to investigate and take necessary actions to protect the child from abuse and neglect.

5. Promoting Resilience and Self-Esteem

a. Encourage Extracurricular Activities

- Involve children in sports, arts, and clubs to promote resilience, build self-esteem, and provide positive social interactions. These activities offer outlets for self-expression and a sense of achievement.

b. Teach Coping Skills

- Educate children on effective coping skills like mindfulness, relaxation techniques, and problem-solving to manage stress and emotional challenges, building emotional resilience.

c. Provide Positive Reinforcement and Validation

- Counteract negative messages from the narcissistic parent by praising efforts, acknowledging strengths, and offering unconditional support. This fosters a positive self-concept and psychological well-being.

Navigating relationship with an NPD patient with poor prognosis

Navigating a relationship with an NPD parent with a poor prognosis is like trying to sail a ship through a hurricane armed only with a cocktail umbrella for protection. Every conversation feels like a delicate dance on a tightrope, except the tightrope is frayed, and your dance partner insists on wearing roller skates. You might find yourself perfecting the art of nodding and smiling, as if you're an extra in a silent movie, just to keep the peace.

Meanwhile, mastering the Houdini-like skill of dodging guilt trips and blame is essential, though you often feel like you're playing an endless game of emotional dodgeball where the balls are made of sticky tar. Remember, maintaining your sanity might involve liberal use of humor, deep breaths, and the occasional strategic retreat to a place where you can roll your eyes in peace.

When facing a poor prognosis for an individual with Narcissistic Personality Disorder (NPD), it's crucial for the spouse, children, and family members to prioritize their own well-being while also providing support and understanding to the NPD patient. Here are some steps they can take to navigate this challenging situation effectively:

1. **Seek Support**: Reach out to trusted friends, family members, or support groups for validation, guidance, and emotional support. Connecting with others who understand your experiences can provide comfort and reassurance during difficult times.

2. **Set Boundaries:** Establish clear and firm boundaries to protect yourself and your children from emotional manipulation, abuse, and harm. Communicate your needs and limits assertively to the NPD patient and enforce consequences if necessary. Setting boundaries is essential for maintaining your emotional and psychological well-being in the relationship.

3. **Focus on Self-Care:** Prioritize self-care practices that promote your physical, emotional, and mental health. Engage in activities that bring you joy, relaxation, and fulfillment, such as exercise, hobbies, meditation, or spending time with loved ones. Taking care of yourself is essential for maintaining resilience and coping with the stress of living with an NPD patient.

4. **Educate Yourself:** Learn more about Narcissistic Personality Disorder and its impact on relationships and families. Understanding the dynamics of NPD can help you develop strategies for managing challenges, setting boundaries, and fostering healthy communication within the family.

5. **Seek Therapy:** Consider individual therapy or family therapy to explore your feelings, develop coping strategies, and improve communication within the family. Therapy provides a safe and supportive environment for processing emotions, gaining insight, and developing skills for managing difficult situations.

6. **Develop a Support Network:** Cultivate relationships with supportive individuals who can offer practical assistance, emotional support, and validation. Having a strong support network can help you navigate the complexities of living with an NPD patient and provide a sense of connection and belonging.

7. **Maintain Perspective:** Remember that you are not responsible for the NPD patient's behavior or recovery. While it's natural to want to help and support them, it's important to prioritize your own well-being and recognize your limitations. You cannot change the NPD patient or force them to seek treatment, but you can focus on taking care of yourself and your children.

8. **Consider Safety:** If you or your children are in immediate danger or experiencing abuse from the NPD patient, prioritize safety above all else.

Develop a safety plan, reach out to local resources for support, and consider seeking legal protection if necessary.

Overall, navigating a poor prognosis for an individual with NPD requires a combination of self-care, boundary-setting, support-seeking, and education. By prioritizing your own well-being and developing effective coping strategies, you can maintain resilience and foster a sense of empowerment in the face of difficult circumstances.

AI as a Compassionate Resource: Supporting NPD Individuals and Their Loved Ones

I as a compassionate resource supporting NPD individuals and their loved ones is like having a virtual therapist who never gets tired, never judges, and has infinite patience – think of it as a digital saint. Imagine an AI with the wisdom of Yoda and the tolerance of a preschool teacher during naptime. For the NPD individual, AI can be a sounding board that listens to their monologues without a hint of eye-rolling or sarcasm, giving them the validation they crave while subtly nudging them towards self-awareness.

For their loved ones, AI is like a secret ally, offering strategies to navigate conversations, deflect blame grenades, and maintain their sanity – all with the humor and empathy of a best friend who never needs a break. It's the ultimate superhero in the realm of emotional support, armed with algorithms and empathy, ready to tackle the complexities of narcissistic dynamics with a smile (albeit a digital one).

Artificial Intelligence (AI) has emerged as a powerful tool in various aspects of mental health support. For individuals with Narcissistic Personality Disorder (NPD) and their loved ones, AI offers unique opportunities to foster empathy, improve interpersonal relationships, and provide essential support.

Building Empathy in NPD Individuals with AI

1. **Therapeutic Interventions**:
    - **AI-Powered Therapy Apps**: Applications like Woebot and Wysa offer cognitive-behavioral therapy (CBT) techniques that can be tailored to help individuals with NPD develop empathy and recognize distorted thinking patterns. These tools provide a safe and non-judgmental space for users to explore their emotions and learn healthier ways to interact with others.
    - **Virtual Reality (VR) Therapy**: VR-based interventions can immerse NPD individuals in scenarios where they experience situations from another person's perspective. This immersive experience can help build empathy by making the emotional experiences of others more tangible.
2. **Compassionate AI Communication**:
    - **Conversational Agents**: AI chatbots can engage individuals with NPD in conversations that encourage reflection on their behavior and its impact on others. These chatbots can provide gentle feedback and promote self-awareness without triggering defensiveness.

- **Emotion Recognition Technology**: AI systems equipped with emotion recognition can help NPD individuals understand and respond appropriately to the emotional cues of others. This technology can be integrated into therapy to reinforce empathetic responses.

Supporting Families and Loved Ones with AI

1. **Educational Resources**:
    - **AI-Driven Educational Platforms**: Platforms like Coursera and Udemy can offer courses specifically designed to educate families about NPD. These courses can include AI-generated interactive content that helps loved ones understand the disorder, recognize patterns of behavior, and learn effective coping strategies.
2. **Emotional Support Tools**:
    - **AI-Powered Counseling Services**: Services like BetterHelp and Talkspace provide access to licensed therapists who can support family members of NPD individuals. AI algorithms can match users with therapists who specialize in dealing with narcissistic relationships, ensuring tailored support.
    - **Support Group Facilitation**: AI can help facilitate online support groups by moderating discussions, suggesting topics, and ensuring a safe and supportive

environment for sharing experiences and advice.

3. **Behavioral Monitoring and Feedback**:
    - **AI-Enabled Wearables**: Wearable devices equipped with AI can monitor physiological indicators of stress and emotional distress in family members. These devices can provide real-time feedback and suggest coping strategies to manage stress and maintain emotional well-being.
    - **Smart Home Devices**: AI-powered home assistants can remind NPD individuals and their families to take breaks, practice mindfulness, or engage in relaxing activities, helping to reduce tension and promote a healthier home environment.

Improving Interpersonal Relationships with AI

1. **Relationship Coaching**:
    - **AI Relationship Coaches**: Digital coaches like ReGain use AI to offer relationship advice and conflict resolution strategies. These coaches can help NPD individuals and their partners navigate challenging conversations and build healthier communication patterns.
    - **Customized Communication Training**: AI can analyze communication patterns and provide personalized feedback on how to improve interactions. This can help NPD

individuals learn to express themselves more constructively and empathetically.

2. **Crisis Management**:

    - **AI Crisis Intervention**: In moments of acute conflict, AI systems can provide immediate support and guidance. For example, AI-driven apps can offer de-escalation techniques and connect users to emergency counseling services if needed.
    - **Predictive Analytics**: AI can analyze behavioral data to predict potential conflicts or emotional crises, allowing families to take proactive steps to mitigate issues before they escalate.

Conclusion

AI-based tools offer promising avenues for supporting individuals with NPD and their loved ones. By fostering empathy, providing educational resources, offering emotional support, and improving interpersonal relationships, AI can play a crucial role in enhancing the quality of life for all involved. While AI cannot replace human compassion, it can certainly augment our ability to understand, support, and connect with one another in meaningful ways.

Case study-The Entrepreneur's Struggle: Raj's Journey with NPD and the Role of AI

Meet Raj

Raj is a 40-year-old successful entrepreneur, husband to Priya, and father to 10-year-old Arjun. Despite his seemingly glamorous life, Raj faces significant challenges due to Narcissistic Personality Disorder (NPD). This condition is marked by a pervasive pattern of grandiosity, a constant need for admiration, and a lack of empathy.

The Struggle with Grandiosity and Self-Perception

Grandiosity is a defining trait for Raj. He views himself as exceptional and deserving of special treatment and admiration. Beneath this facade, however, lies a fragile self-esteem, perpetually seeking validation from others. This need for admiration drives Raj to maintain his grandiose self-image at all costs.

The Emotional Disconnect and Lack of Empathy

Raj's outward confidence contrasts sharply with his emotional struggles. His interactions with Priya and Arjun often lack emotional intimacy and empathy. Raj finds it difficult to connect with others' emotions, leading to frequent conflicts and misunderstandings within his family.

The Burden of Vulnerability and Shame

Beneath Raj's grandiose exterior is a deep-seated vulnerability and shame. He fears criticism and rejection, striving to protect his fragile self-esteem from perceived threats. This fear drives Raj's defensive behaviors, manifesting as rage and aggression when his self-image is challenged.

Navigating Relationships and Family Dynamics

Raj's NPD significantly impacts his family life. His need for control and admiration leads to conflicts with Priya, creating a rift between them. Arjun, their son, experiences emotional neglect and manipulation, further complicating family dynamics. Raj's NPD poses barriers to forming genuine relationships, leaving him feeling isolated and misunderstood.

Seeking Understanding and Support

Despite these challenges, Raj is not without hope. Through therapy and support groups, he seeks to gain insight into his condition and develop healthier coping mechanisms. Understanding his perspective and the impact of his behaviors on his family are crucial first steps towards healing and self-awareness.

The Role of AI in Supporting NPD Individuals and Their Loved Ones

Building Empathy with AI-Based Tools

AI-based tools can play a pivotal role in helping individuals with NPD, like Raj, develop empathy. Advanced AI systems can simulate emotional responses and provide real-time feedback during interactions, helping individuals recognize and understand emotional cues. This can aid in improving emotional intelligence and fostering empathy.

Enhancing Interpersonal Relationships

AI-driven platforms can offer personalized therapy sessions that adapt to the individual's emotional state, providing strategies to manage narcissistic tendencies. These platforms can also facilitate communication skills training, helping individuals with NPD learn to engage in more empathetic and meaningful conversations with their loved ones.

Supporting Families and Loved Ones

For families like Raj's, AI technology can offer valuable support. AI-based applications can provide resources and strategies for managing relationships with NPD individuals.

These tools can offer guided exercises for setting healthy boundaries, effective communication techniques, and coping mechanisms to handle emotional stress.

AI in Therapy and Support Groups

AI-powered virtual therapists can provide accessible and affordable mental health support, offering continuous monitoring and feedback. These virtual therapists can help NPD individuals track their progress, practice empathy-building exercises, and receive instant support during emotional crises. Additionally, AI can facilitate support groups by connecting individuals and families dealing with NPD, providing a platform for sharing experiences and advice.

Conclusion: A Journey of Self-Discovery

Raj's journey with NPD underscores the complexities of living with a personality disorder. Through introspection, therapy, and the innovative support of AI-based tools, he begins to unravel the layers of his condition, seeking understanding and acceptance. By integrating AI into his journey, Raj takes significant steps towards improving his relationships and fostering a more empathetic and supportive family environment. This case highlights the potential of AI to transform the lives of individuals with NPD and their loved ones, offering new pathways to healing and self-discovery.

Chapter 8:
Embracing Change: AI as a Catalyst for Lasting Transformation

As we venture deeper into the realm of personal growth, this chapter explores how artificial intelligence can act as a catalyst for lasting transformation, particularly for individuals navigating the complexities of narcissistic personality patterns. The journey toward change is neither linear nor simple, but the integration of AI tools and techniques offers a unique opportunity to facilitate and accelerate this process.

AI-Driven Habit Formation and Change

Habits play a crucial role in shaping our behaviors, thoughts, and ultimately, our personalities. For those striving to overcome narcissistic traits, the formation of new, healthier habits is essential. AI can significantly aid in this process through personalized habit-tracking apps and platforms that not only monitor progress but also provide tailored suggestions based on individual behavior patterns. These tools leverage data analytics and machine learning to identify optimal intervention points, making habit change more manageable and less daunting.

Personalized Learning and Growth Pathways

One of the challenges in addressing narcissistic personality patterns lies in the diverse manifestations of these traits. AI's capacity for personalization allows for the creation of bespoke learning and growth pathways that address the specific needs and challenges of an individual. Through adaptive learning systems, AI can curate content, exercises, and reflection activities that resonate with the user's unique experiences, promoting deeper insights and more impactful growth.

Enhancing Self-Awareness Through Feedback Loops

A critical component of personal transformation is enhanced self-awareness. AI technologies, especially those incorporating feedback mechanisms, can provide objective, real-time insights into one's behaviors, emotional states, and interaction patterns. For example, wearable technology can monitor physiological responses to stress or emotional triggers, offering immediate feedback that helps users recognize and adjust their responses. Similarly, AI-enhanced journaling apps can analyze written reflections for emotional content and patterns, encouraging deeper self-exploration and awareness.

Overcoming Resistance Through AI Engagement

Change, especially for individuals with narcissistic tendencies, can be met with resistance, whether due to fear, denial, or discomfort with vulnerability. AI's non-judgmental, neutral stance offers a unique advantage in engaging users in a way that feels safe and non-threatening. Gamification elements, interactive exercises, and virtual AI companions can make the process of self-discovery and change more engaging and less intimidating, gently nudging users out of their comfort zones.

Long-Term Progress Monitoring

Long-term progress monitoring for Narcissistic Personality Disorder (NPD) patients involves utilizing AI algorithms to track treatment outcomes over time. AI aids therapists in assessing the effectiveness of therapy interventions, adjusting strategies, and providing personalized feedback based on real-time data. Utilize AI algorithms to track long-term progress and outcomes of therapeutic interventions for individuals with NPD, enabling therapists to adjust treatment strategies based on real-time data

Virtual Therapeutic Environments

Virtual Therapeutic Environments offer immersive, safe spaces where individuals with Narcissistic Personality Disorder (NPD) can practice social interactions, empathy, and self-reflection. Through AI-guided simulations, patients can gradually learn adaptive behaviours, leading to lasting changes in their interpersonal relationships and self-awareness

Sustaining Transformation through Community and Support

Finally, the journey of transformation is not one to be undertaken in isolation. AI can facilitate connection to supportive communities and resources, matching individuals with peer groups, mentors, or therapists who can provide encouragement and guidance. Online platforms powered by AI can create safe, anonymous spaces for sharing experiences and strategies, fostering a sense of belonging and support that is crucial for lasting change.

In embracing AI as a tool for personal transformation, we recognize its potential to act as a bridge between current limitations and future possibilities. The path toward overcoming narcissistic traits and fostering a more empathetic, self-aware, and connected self is enriched and potentially accelerated by these technological advancements. As we look ahead, the promise of AI in personal development is not just in the tools and technologies themselves, but in their capacity to empower individuals to take meaningful steps toward lasting change.

Limitations Of Behaviour Modification With AI For Lasting Behaviour Change

Using AI for behavior modification has its limitations when it comes to achieving lasting behavior change:

1. **Lack of Human Element:** AI may lack the empathy and understanding needed to address the root causes of behavior, which are often deeply personal and complex.

2. **Dependency on Data:** AI relies heavily on data, which may not always accurately capture the nuances of human behavior or the context in which it occurs.

3. **Over-reliance on Reinforcement**: Behavior modification with AI often relies on reinforcement techniques, which may not address underlying psychological or emotional factors contributing to the behavior.

4. **Resistance to Change:** People may resist behavior modification efforts imposed by AI, particularly if they feel it intrudes on their autonomy or privacy.

5. **Ethical Concerns**: There are ethical concerns regarding the use of AI for behavior modification, including issues related to consent, manipulation, and potential harm.

6. **Limited Scope**: AI may be limited in its ability to address multifaceted behaviors that are influenced by a variety of factors, such as social, cultural, and environmental influences.

7. **Generalization**: AI algorithms may struggle to generalize behavior change strategies across different individuals or contexts, leading to less effective outcomes.

8. **Maintenance of Change**: Even if AI successfully initiates behavior change, sustaining it over the long term may be challenging without ongoing support and reinforcement.

Chapter 9:
The Future of AI and Personal Development: Ethical Considerations and Beyond

As we approach the horizon of personal growth through the lens of artificial intelligence, this chapter addresses the future implications, ethical considerations, and potential advancements in the intersection of AI and personal development, especially for individuals with narcissistic personality patterns. The integration of AI in personal transformation journeys presents not only immense possibilities but also significant responsibilities and ethical dilemmas.

Ethical Use of AI in Personal Development

The ethical use of AI technology in personal development, particularly for sensitive areas such as mental health and personality modification, requires careful consideration. Issues such as data privacy, consent, and the potential for misuse of personal information are paramount. There must be transparent mechanisms that ensure AI applications in personal development adhere to the highest standards of privacy, confidentiality, and user respect, safeguarding against exploitation or manipulation.

Legal And Regulatory Challenges In AI-Driven Personal Development

Legal and regulatory challenges in AI-driven personal development arise due to the intersection of AI technologies with individual well-being and personal growth. These challenges include:

1. **Data Privacy and Protection**: Ensuring compliance with data protection laws and regulations to safeguard the privacy of personal data collected and processed by AI systems.
2. **Ethical Use of AI Algorithms**: Addressing ethical concerns regarding the fairness, transparency, and accountability of AI algorithms used in personal development applications.
3. **Informed Consent and User Rights:** Establishing mechanisms for obtaining informed consent from users and ensuring that individuals retain control over their personal data and AI-generated insights.
4. **Legal Liability and Accountability:** Clarifying legal liability frameworks to determine

accountability in cases of harm or adverse effects resulting from AI-driven personal development interventions.
5. **Regulatory Compliance and Standardization**: Developing regulatory frameworks and industry standards to govern the development, deployment, and use of AI technologies in personal development while promoting innovation and protecting user interests.
6. **International Cooperation and Governance**: Fostering international cooperation and collaboration to address cross-border legal and regulatory challenges and ensure harmonization of AI policies and standards.

These challenges underscore the need for proactive measures to navigate the legal and regulatory landscape of AI-driven personal development effectively.

Bias and Fairness

AI systems are only as unbiased as the data they are trained on. Therefore, ensuring that AI tools for personal growth are free from bias and equitable in their functionality across different demographics is crucial. This includes attention to how narcissistic traits are understood and addressed across cultures, genders, and socio-economic backgrounds, preventing the perpetuation of stereotypes or the exclusion of certain groups from the benefits of AI-driven personal development.

The Role of Human Oversight

While AI can offer personalized insights and support, the role of human oversight cannot be understated. Mental health professionals, ethicists, and AI developers must work collaboratively to oversee AI applications in personal growth, ensuring they are used appropriately and complement traditional therapeutic approaches. This collaboration is vital for addressing complex personality patterns like narcissism, where the nuances of human behavior and emotion require a level of understanding and empathy beyond current AI capabilities.

Future Directions in AI and Narcissistic Personality Development

Looking forward, the evolution of AI holds promising advancements for personal development, especially in understanding and addressing narcissistic personality patterns. Enhanced natural language processing and machine learning models could offer deeper insights into emotional intelligence and empathy, providing more nuanced feedback and intervention strategies. Additionally, augmented reality (AR) and further advancements in VR could offer even more immersive experiences for empathy training and social skill development.

Societal Implications and the Path Forward

As AI becomes more integrated into personal development efforts, its societal implications—ranging from accessibility to the impact on traditional therapy and counseling professions—must be thoughtfully considered. Ensuring equitable access to these technologies is essential to avoid widening the gap in mental health resources and support.

Moreover, as we venture into this future, ongoing dialogue between AI developers, mental health professionals, ethicists, and users is crucial to navigate the ethical, practical, and emotional complexities of using AI in personal growth. By prioritizing ethical considerations and human values, we can harness the potential of AI to offer transformative support for individuals seeking to overcome narcissistic personality patterns and embark on a journey of self-improvement and interpersonal connection.

In closing, the journey of integrating AI into personal development, particularly for navigating the complexities of narcissism, is filled with potential and pitfalls alike. As we chart this course, our collective responsibility is to guide this integration with compassion, ethics, and a forward-looking vision, ensuring that the technology that has the power to change us does so in ways that uplift, empower, and unite.

Challenges in the Future of AI in the management of NPD

In the future, AI faces several challenges in the management of Narcissistic Personality Disorder (NPD):

1. **Accuracy of Diagnosis**: AI algorithms need to accurately diagnose NPD based on complex behavioral patterns, which may be challenging due to the variability in symptoms and individual differences.

2. **Ethical Considerations:** There are ethical concerns surrounding the use of AI in diagnosing and treating mental

health disorders, including issues of privacy, consent, and potential misuse of personal data.

3. **Limited Understanding of Human Behavior:** AI may struggle to fully understand the intricacies of human behavior, particularly the underlying psychological factors that contribute to NPD.

4. **Tailored Treatment Approaches**: Developing AI-driven treatment approaches that are tailored to the unique needs of individuals with NPD requires a deep understanding of both the disorder and the nuances of human psychology.

5. **Therapeutic Alliance**: Building a therapeutic alliance between individuals with NPD and AI-driven systems may be challenging, as it requires trust, empathy, and understanding, which are typically associated with human interactions.

6. **Long-Term Efficacy:** Ensuring the long-term efficacy of AI-driven interventions for NPD requires ongoing monitoring, adaptation, and support, which may be difficult to sustain outside of traditional therapeutic settings.

7. **Integration with Existing Systems:** Integrating AI-driven tools for NPD management into existing healthcare systems poses logistical challenges, including compatibility with electronic health records, regulatory compliance, and clinician acceptance.

8. **Addressing Societal Stigma**: Overcoming societal stigma surrounding mental health disorders, including NPD, is essential for the widespread adoption and acceptance of AI-driven interventions in this domain.

Chapter 10:
Navigating the Journey Ahead: Empowering Individuals and Communities

In this chapter of our exploration into the transformative potential of artificial intelligence for individuals with narcissistic personality patterns, we look toward the journey ahead. This future is not solely about the individuals undergoing transformation but also about how these changes can empower broader communities. The application of AI in personal development, particularly in the context of narcissism, holds the promise of fostering more empathetic, understanding, and cohesive societies.

Empowering Individuals for Sustainable Change

The empowerment of individuals to take charge of their personal growth journey is a cornerstone of sustainable change. AI tools and applications offer unprecedented opportunities for self-reflection, learning, and transformation on a deeply personal level. By providing tailored insights and interventions, AI can help individuals understand the root causes of their behaviors and attitudes, guiding them toward healthier patterns of thought and interaction. This empowerment extends beyond personal benefit, as the changes in one person ripple out to influence their relationships and communities.

Strengthening Community Bonds

As individuals engage with AI-driven personal development tools, the potential for these technologies to strengthen community bonds becomes evident. Communities, both online and offline, can benefit from shared experiences and resources, creating a supportive environment for growth and healing. AI can facilitate the creation of these supportive networks, connecting individuals with similar growth goals and challenges, and enabling the exchange of strategies, successes, and support. Such connections not only reinforce individual efforts but also contribute to a culture of empathy and understanding within communities.

The Role of AI in Education and Awareness

The integration of AI into educational settings offers another pathway to empower communities. By incorporating AI-driven modules on empathy, emotional intelligence, and healthy interpersonal skills into educational curricula, we can nurture these essential qualities from a young age. For adults, continuous education platforms can utilize AI to offer personalized learning experiences focused on personal development and mental health awareness. Such initiatives can play a crucial role in demystifying narcissistic personality patterns and promoting a more nuanced understanding of these behaviors within society.

Ethical and Inclusive Development of AI Tools

As we embrace the future of AI in personal and communal development, the importance of ethical, inclusive, and participatory design processes cannot be overstated. Involving a diverse range of voices, including those with lived experiences of narcissism, in the development of AI tools ensures that these technologies are sensitive to the nuances of human psychology and interpersonal dynamics. This approach not only enhances the effectiveness of AI applications but also ensures they serve the broadest possible spectrum of individuals and communities.

Looking Forward: A Collaborative Vision for the Future

The journey ahead requires a collaborative vision, one that embraces the complexities of human nature while leveraging the innovative potential of AI. By fostering dialogue among technologists, mental health professionals, ethicists, and the communities they serve, we can navigate the challenges and opportunities presented by AI in personal development. Together, we can build a future where technology not only supports individual growth but also enriches the fabric of our communities.

In this future, the role of AI in addressing narcissistic personality patterns is just one facet of a broader movement toward harnessing technology for the greater good. As we close this book, let us carry forward the message that while technology has the power to transform, it is our shared humanity that guides this transformation toward a more empathetic, understanding, and connected world.

Case Study: Mrs. Gupta - A Female Narcissist

Background:

Mrs. Gupta is a 52-year-old woman residing in Mumbai, India. She has been married to Mr. Gupta for 30 years. Throughout their marriage, Mrs. Gupta has exhibited traits consistent with Narcissistic Personality Disorder (NPD). She constantly seeks admiration, lacks empathy for others, and manipulates situations to serve her own needs.

Behavior Patterns:

Mrs. Gupta consistently treats her husband, Mr. Gupta, like a servant rather than a partner. She demands constant attention and validation from him, often belittling his accomplishments and controlling his actions. Despite Mr. Gupta's efforts to please her, Mrs. Gupta remains unsatisfied and continues to manipulate him emotionally and financially.

Financial Exploitation:

Over the years, Mrs. Gupta has systematically squeezed all of Mr. Gupta's financial resources for her own benefit. She insists on extravagant purchases, expensive vacations, and luxurious lifestyle choices, all funded by Mr. Gupta's hard-earned money. Despite their financial struggles, Mrs. Gupta shows no remorse for her actions and continues to demand more from her husband.

Impact on Mr. Gupta:

Mr. Gupta's self-esteem and mental well-being have been severely affected by his wife's behavior. He feels trapped in a relationship where his needs are constantly overlooked, and his efforts go unappreciated. Despite seeking support from friends and family, Mr. Gupta struggles to break free from the cycle of manipulation and control perpetuated by his wife.

Potential Interventions:

1. **Therapy and Counseling:** Mr. Gupta could benefit from individual therapy to address the emotional toll of living with a narcissistic partner. Additionally, couples therapy may help improve communication and set boundaries within the relationship.

2. **Financial Planning:** Seeking assistance from a financial advisor could help Mr. Gupta regain control over his finances and protect his assets from further exploitation by his wife.

3. **Legal Support**: Exploring legal options, such as divorce or separation, may be necessary to protect Mr. Gupta's interests and ensure his well-being in the long term.

4. Community Support: Joining support groups or seeking guidance from organizations specializing in domestic abuse and narcissistic relationships can provide Mr. Gupta with a sense of solidarity and validation.

This case study highlights the complexities involved in managing relationships with individuals exhibiting narcissistic traits and underscores the need for comprehensive support systems to address the multifaceted challenges faced by victims of narcissistic abuse.

Chapter 11:
Beyond the Book: Implementing Change in the Real World

As we venture beyond the confines of this book, Chapter 10 is dedicated to translating the insights and strategies discussed into tangible actions and changes in the real world. The journey of utilizing artificial intelligence to address narcissistic personality patterns, and more broadly, to foster personal growth, is not confined to theoretical exploration. It demands practical application, ongoing evaluation, and a commitment to adapting these technologies to meet the evolving needs of individuals and communities.

Practical Implementation of AI Tools

The first step toward implementing change involves the practical integration of AI tools into everyday life and clinical practice. For individuals, this might mean choosing AI-driven apps or platforms that focus on self-awareness, empathy development, or stress management. For mental health professionals, it involves incorporating AI-assisted diagnostics, therapy enhancements, and patient monitoring into their practice, all while maintaining ethical standards and personalized care.

Creating Accessible and Inclusive AI Solutions

To ensure the benefits of AI in personal development are widely accessible, it's crucial to address barriers to technology access. This includes making AI tools available across a range of devices and platforms, offering low-cost or free options, and ensuring that these tools are user-friendly for people with varying levels of tech-savvy. Equally important is the development of AI solutions that are inclusive, taking into account diverse cultural, linguistic, and socio-economic contexts to make personal growth opportunities truly universal.

Building Partnerships for Wider Impact

The path to implementing change on a broader scale involves building partnerships between technology developers, mental health professionals, educational institutions, and community organizations. These partnerships can facilitate the sharing of resources, knowledge, and best practices, ensuring that AI tools for personal development are grounded in scientific research, ethical principles, and an understanding of the complex dynamics of human behavior.

Fostering a Culture of Continuous Learning and Adaptation

As AI technologies evolve, so too must our approaches to integrating them into personal development efforts. This requires a culture of continuous learning and adaptation, where feedback from users and new scientific findings are regularly incorporated into the design and deployment of AI tools. By remaining open to change and committed to improvement, we can ensure that these technologies continue to serve the best interests of those seeking to grow and change.

Advocating for Ethical Standards and Regulation

Finally, advocating for the establishment and enforcement of ethical standards and regulations in the use of AI for personal development is paramount. This includes privacy protection, data security, and the prevention of harm. As we move forward, it is the responsibility of all stakeholders involved in the development and use of AI tools to champion these standards and ensure that the technology is used in ways that enhance, rather than undermine, human dignity and well-being.

Challenges to implementing changes in the real world of repairing from narcissistic abuse

Implementing changes in the real world after experiencing narcissistic abuse can be incredibly challenging due to various factors:

1. **Psychological Impact**: Narcissistic abuse can cause deep psychological wounds, making it difficult to trust oneself and

others. Overcoming these internal barriers is a significant challenge.

2. **Gaslighting**: Narcissists often employ gaslighting techniques to manipulate and control their victims, leading to confusion and self-doubt. Recognizing and overcoming gaslighting tactics can be daunting.

3. **Isolation:** Narcissists often isolate their victims from friends, family, and support networks, leaving them feeling alone and without resources. Rebuilding a support system is crucial but can be challenging.

4. **Fear of Repercussions:** Victims may fear retaliation or further abuse if they attempt to break free from the narcissist's control. Overcoming this fear and taking steps to protect oneself requires courage and determination.

5. **Financial Dependence:** Narcissists may exert control over their victims by controlling finances or creating dependence. Breaking free from financial entanglements can be complex and daunting.

6. **Trauma Bonding**: Victims of narcissistic abuse often develop a strong attachment to their abuser, making it difficult to leave or make changes. Breaking free from this trauma bond requires time, support, and self-awareness.

7. **Rebuilding Self-Esteem:** Narcissistic abuse can severely damage self-esteem and self-worth. Rebuilding a positive self-image and sense of worthiness takes time and effort.

8. **Legal and Practical Considerations**: In some cases, implementing changes may involve legal proceedings such as divorce or restraining orders. Navigating the legal system and practical logistics can be overwhelming.

Despite these challenges, it's important to remember that healing and recovery are possible with time, support, and self-care. Seeking therapy, joining support groups, and practicing self-compassion can all aid in the journey toward healing from narcissistic abuse.

Conclusion

As we conclude this book, it is clear that the journey of integrating AI into the process of personal and communal development is just beginning. The potential of artificial intelligence to support individuals in overcoming narcissistic personality patterns and achieving personal growth is vast, but realizing this potential requires concerted effort, ethical diligence, and a commitment to human-centered design. By taking the insights and strategies outlined in this book and applying them in the real world, we can embark on a transformative journey that leverages the best of what AI has to offer, creating a future where technology and humanity collaborate for the betterment of all.

Chapter 12:
A Call to Action: Mobilizing a Community for Change

In the final chapter of our exploration, we shift our focus from the theoretical and practical applications of AI in personal development to a broader, more encompassing perspective—a call to action for individuals, professionals, and societies at large. This call to action is not just about embracing AI technologies but about fostering a global community committed to using these tools responsibly and ethically for the betterment of humanity.

Empowering Individuals with Knowledge and Tools

The journey starts with individuals. Empowering people with the knowledge and tools to understand and work on narcissistic personality patterns—or any personal growth challenge—is critical. This involves not only making AI tools more accessible but also educating the public on how to use these technologies effectively and safely. Workshops, online courses, and informational resources can demystify AI and encourage its integration into daily routines for personal reflection, growth, and healing.

Encouraging Professional Engagement and Development

Mental health professionals, educators, and AI developers play a pivotal role in this ecosystem. Encouraging these professionals to engage with AI technologies, understand their applications and limitations, and contribute to their development can ensure that these tools are both effective and deeply compassionate. Professional development programs, interdisciplinary conferences, and collaborative research projects can bridge the gap between technology and human-centric care.

Fostering Ethical AI Development

As we embrace the potential of AI, the imperative for ethical development and application becomes paramount. This involves creating transparent, participatory processes that involve stakeholders from diverse backgrounds in the design, testing, and rollout of AI solutions. Establishing ethical guidelines, privacy protections, and standards for inclusivity and accessibility ensures that AI technologies serve the diverse needs and rights of all individuals.

Building Community Support Systems

The power of community cannot be understated. Building support systems that leverage AI for public awareness, education, and mutual aid can transform the landscape of personal development. Online forums, peer support groups, and community-based initiatives can provide spaces for individuals to share their journeys, challenges, and successes, fostering a culture of empathy, understanding, and collective growth.

Advocating for Policy and Societal Change

The broader adoption and ethical use of AI in personal development also require advocacy for policy and societal change. This includes lobbying for the responsible regulation of AI technologies, advocating for the integration of AI into public health initiatives, and promoting digital literacy as a fundamental skill in education systems. By influencing policy and societal norms, we can create an environment that nurtures personal growth and respects the dignity and rights of every individual.

Conclusion: A Collective Journey Forward

This book has navigated the complexities of narcissism, personal growth, and the potential of AI as a tool for transformative change. As we conclude, we recognize that the true potential of AI in personal development lies not in the technology itself but in our ability to harness it for the greater good. This final chapter is a call to action for everyone—individuals, professionals, and communities—to engage with AI technologies thoughtfully, ethically, and compassionately.

As we step forward, let us do so as a global community committed to using AI to enhance our understanding of ourselves and others, to heal and grow, and to build a more empathetic and understanding world. The journey ahead is a collective one, filled with challenges, opportunities, and the promise of a future where technology and humanity walk hand in hand toward a brighter, more inclusive horizon.

Chapter 13:
Envisioning the Future: AI and the Evolution of Personal Development

As we close this comprehensive exploration into the nexus of artificial intelligence and personal development, particularly through the lens of navigating narcissistic personality patterns, it's essential to cast our gaze forward. This chapter is not just a conclusion but an invitation to imagine the future—a future where AI doesn't merely assist in managing specific personality traits but profoundly transforms the landscape of personal growth and mental health care.

The Next Generation of AI Tools

Looking ahead, we envision the next generation of AI tools becoming even more sophisticated and nuanced in their understanding of human emotions, behaviors, and needs. These advanced systems will likely offer more personalized feedback and support, adapting in real-time to the user's emotional state, progress, and changing goals. Imagine AI that can not only recognize when you're feeling down or particularly narcissistic but also suggest the most effective interventions tailored to that exact moment, blending cognitive-behavioral strategies with personalized care.

AI as a Catalyst for Deeper Self-Understanding

The future of AI in personal development promises a journey towards deeper self-understanding and self-awareness. As AI technologies become more integrated into our daily lives, they will provide continuous opportunities for reflection and growth. This constant companion could help individuals recognize patterns in their behavior or thinking that are invisible to them but evident to an objective observer. In this way, AI has the potential to mirror back to us our true selves, warts and all, encouraging a deeper introspection and a more authentic journey of self-improvement.

Bridging the Gap Between AI and Human Connection

A crucial evolution we foresee is the bridging of the current gap between AI and genuine human connection. Future developments will likely focus on how AI can facilitate stronger, healthier interpersonal relationships. This includes AI that coaches individuals on empathy, active listening, and constructive communication, especially valuable for those navigating narcissistic tendencies. Such tools could act as a bridge, enhancing human connections rather than replacing them, fostering a world where technology enhances our humanity.

The Role of AI in Creating a More Empathetic Society

The broad adoption of AI in personal development also has the potential to contribute to a more empathetic and understanding society. As individuals become more self-aware and empathetic, these qualities can ripple outwards, affecting societal norms and behaviors. AI could play a significant role in education, from early childhood development to ongoing adult education, emphasizing emotional intelligence, empathy, and mental well-being as foundational skills for the future.

Ethical Considerations and Human Agency

As we dream of the future, the ethical considerations of AI integration into personal development become even more significant. Ensuring that these technologies enhance human agency rather than diminish it is paramount. This future hinges on developing AI in a way that prioritizes privacy, consent, and inclusivity, ensuring that the benefits of these technologies are accessible to all, regardless of background, economic status, or geography.

A Collaborative Future

Finally, the future we envision is one of collaboration—not just between humans and AI but among developers, psychologists, ethicists, policymakers, and the public. This collaborative approach ensures that AI development is guided by a diverse array of perspectives, fostering technologies that truly meet human needs and enhance our collective well-being.

In Conclusion

As we conclude this journey through the potential of AI in addressing narcissistic personality patterns and fostering personal growth, it's clear that we stand on the brink of a new era. This future, filled with promise and potential challenges, invites us to imagine a world where AI not only understands the complexities of human psychology but also enriches our lives in profound and enduring ways. It's a future that we can shape together, with each discovery, each development, and each step forward bringing us closer to realizing the full potential of AI as a partner in our journey towards personal and societal growth.

Management through Collaborative Approach

The management of individuals with narcissistic personality patterns can significantly benefit from a collaborative team effort, involving a multidisciplinary approach that encompasses various professionals such as psychologists, psychiatrists, counselors, social workers, and possibly even AI specialists when considering the integration of technology into treatment plans. This collaborative approach offers a comprehensive, multi-faceted strategy for understanding, supporting, and facilitating change in individuals with narcissistic tendencies. Here are several key aspects of how collaborative team effort plays a crucial role:

1. Comprehensive Assessment

- Diverse Perspectives: Different professionals bring varied perspectives to the assessment process, which can lead to a more comprehensive understanding of the individual's behaviors, thoughts, and emotions.

- Holistic View: By combining insights from various fields, the team can develop a holistic view of the person, considering not just psychological aspects but also social, physical, and technological influences.

2. Integrated Treatment Plan

- Personalized Approaches: A collaborative team can tailor treatment plans to the individual's specific needs, incorporating various therapeutic modalities like cognitive-behavioral therapy (CBT), dialectical behavior therapy (DBT), and psychoeducation.

- Consistency and Coordination: Coordinated care ensures that all team members are aligned on the treatment goals and approaches, reducing the risk of contradictory advice and reinforcing the treatment framework.

3. Continuous Support and Monitoring

- Round-the-Clock Support: Collaboration among team members can provide the individual with access to continuous support, essential for navigating the complexities of narcissistic personality patterns.

- Adaptive Strategies: As the individual progresses, the team can quickly adapt treatment plans based on real-time feedback and evolving needs.

4. Addressing Comorbid Conditions

- Expertise in Comorbidity: Narcissistic personality patterns often co-occur with other mental health issues, such as depression or anxiety. A multidisciplinary team can address these comorbid conditions more effectively than a single practitioner.

- Integrated Care: Treating the individual holistically, considering both narcissistic patterns and any comorbid conditions, can lead to better overall outcomes.

5. Enhancing Treatment Engagement

- Trust and Rapport: Different team members may connect with the individual in unique ways, helping to build trust and rapport, which are crucial for engaging someone with narcissistic traits in therapy.

- Mitigating Resistance: A collaborative approach can also help in creatively addressing and mitigating the resistance to treatment often exhibited by individuals with narcissistic personality patterns.

6. Utilizing Technological Advances

- AI and Digital Tools: Integrating AI tools and digital platforms, under the guidance of technology specialists in collaboration with mental health professionals, can offer innovative ways to support treatment, such as through monitoring mood and behavior, providing personalized feedback, and enhancing self-awareness.

Conclusion

A collaborative team effort in managing narcissistic personality patterns fosters a comprehensive, nuanced, and flexible approach to treatment. It leverages the strengths and specialized knowledge of various professionals, enhancing the efficacy of interventions and supporting the individual's journey towards healthier ways of relating to themselves and others.

How AI can help in Managing Narcissistic Personality Patterns

While specific case studies detailing the use of AI to manage narcissistic personality patterns in females are not directly available in the public domain due to privacy and ethical considerations, we can discuss hypothetical scenarios based on existing AI applications in mental health. These scenarios can illustrate how AI might be used to support treatment and management in individuals exhibiting narcissistic traits, focusing on personalized approaches, behavior modification, and emotional understanding.

CASE STUDIES

Case Study 1: Virtual Reality (VR) Therapy for Empathy Development

Background: Jaya is a 34-year-old female diagnosed with narcissistic personality disorder (NPD), struggling with empathy and understanding others' perspectives. Traditional therapy has made some progress, but her therapist wants to enhance her ability to empathize with others.

Intervention: Jaya is introduced to a VR therapy program designed to simulate social situations where she can practice responding to others' emotions and needs. The AI-driven program adjusts scenarios based on her responses, gradually increasing complexity and introducing more nuanced emotional cues.

Outcome: Over several months, Jaya reports a noticeable improvement in her ability to understand and react to others' feelings. Her therapist also notes a decrease in narcissistic behaviors during sessions, indicating a positive shift in Jaya's interpersonal skills.

Case Study 2: AI-Powered Mood and Behavior Tracking

Background: Sarah, a 28-year-old with strong narcissistic traits, often lacks awareness of her mood fluctuations and their impact on her behavior towards others. Her counselor suggests incorporating technology to increase her self-awareness.

Intervention: Sarah starts using an AI-powered app that tracks her mood through daily check-ins and analyzes her text messages and social media posts for emotional tone. The app provides feedback on patterns in her mood and communication style, highlighting potential areas for improvement.

Outcome: Sarah gains insights into how her mood influences her interactions with friends and family. Armed with this knowledge, she begins to recognize the early signs of negative mood shifts and takes steps to address them before they affect her behavior.

Case Study 3: Personalized Cognitive Behavioral Therapy (CBT) via AI Chatbot

Background: Lakshmi, a 40-year-old executive with narcissistic personality traits, finds it challenging to attend regular therapy sessions due to her busy schedule. She seeks an alternative that fits her lifestyle.

Intervention: Lakshmi decides to try an AI chatbot designed to deliver personalized CBT sessions. The chatbot guides her through exercises aimed at challenging her narcissistic thoughts and behaviors, providing immediate feedback and suggestions for alternative approaches.

Outcome: The convenience and immediacy of the chatbot enable Lakshmi to engage with therapeutic exercises more consistently. Over time, she notices a reduction in her need for admiration and an increase in her capacity for self-reflection and personal growth.

Conclusion

These case studies illustrate the potential of AI to complement traditional therapies in managing narcissistic personality patterns. By offering personalized, accessible, and innovative interventions, AI can play a crucial role in supporting individuals in their journey towards healthier interpersonal relationships and improved emotional well-being. However, it's essential to recognize that AI tools should supplement, not replace, the expertise of mental health professionals.

Case Study: The Kapoors - Navigating Narcissistic Family Dynamics Through Open Communication

Background:

The Kapoor family consisted of Anirudh and Rohan, a married couple in their mid-30s, and their two children. Anirudh came from a family with strong narcissistic patterns, characterized by a lack of empathy, a need for admiration, and difficulty maintaining healthy relationships. Growing up in this environment, Anirudh had unconsciously adopted some of these traits, which began to surface more prominently after marriage and the birth of their children. Rohan, noticing the strain on their marriage and family life, suggested seeking professional help.

Intervention:

- The couple embarked on a journey of therapy, both individually and as a couple, with a focus on understanding and addressing the impact of narcissistic family patterns on their relationship. The key interventions included:
- Individual Therapy for Anirudh: Anirudh engaged in individual therapy sessions to work on self-awareness, particularly regarding traits inherited from the family dynamics. The therapist used cognitive-behavioral therapy (CBT) to help Anirudh identify and challenge distorted perceptions and behaviors learned from their family.
- Couples Therapy: The couple attended therapy sessions together, focusing on enhancing communication, empathy, and understanding. The therapist introduced exercises designed to improve active listening skills and validate each other's feelings, aiming to break the cycle of narcissistic behavior patterns affecting their relationship.
- Family Therapy: To better navigate parenting and reduce the transmission of narcissistic traits to their children, the Kapoors participated in family therapy. This helped them establish healthier family dynamics and more effective communication strategies.
- Educational Workshops: Both Anirudh and Rohan attended workshops on understanding narcissism and its effects on families. These workshops provided them with tools to recognize and address unhealthy behaviors, facilitating a more supportive and nurturing family environment.

Outcome:

Over the course of two years, the Kapoors noticed significant improvements in their relationship and family life:

- Improved Communication: Anirudh and Rohan developed stronger communication skills, enabling them to express their needs and feelings more openly and constructively.

- Increased Empathy: Anirudh showed considerable progress in demonstrating empathy and understanding towards Rohan and the children, a stark contrast to the previously observed narcissistic traits.

- Healthier Family Dynamics: The couple established new family routines and traditions that emphasized mutual respect, cooperation, and emotional support.

- Enhanced Parenting Skills: By actively working to break the cycle of narcissism, Anirudh and Rohan became more attentive and responsive parents, fostering a loving and secure environment for their children.

Conclusion:

The Kapoors' journey highlights the profound impact that understanding and addressing narcissistic family patterns can have on saving and strengthening a marriage and family life. Through dedicated therapeutic work and a commitment to change, individuals and families can overcome the challenges posed by these complex dynamics, paving the way for healthier, more fulfilling relationships.

Case Study: Mayank's Journey to Job Stability Through AI-Assisted Interventions

Background:

Mayank, a 29-year-old with pronounced narcissistic personality patterns, faced recurring challenges in sustaining employment. Despite his skills and qualifications, interpersonal conflicts, a lack of empathy, and difficulty accepting feedback led to repeated job losses. Recognizing the need for change, Mayank explored new approaches to manage his behavior, particularly through AI-assisted interventions.

Intervention:

Mayank's journey began with a comprehensive evaluation by a team of mental health professionals who collaborated with AI specialists. This multidisciplinary team designed a personalized intervention plan, leveraging AI technologies to address Mayank's specific challenges in the workplace.

1. AI-Powered Behavioral Therapy App:

- Mayank was introduced to an AI-powered app designed to improve emotional intelligence and empathy. The app used daily scenarios and role-play exercises to simulate workplace interactions, offering real-time feedback on Mayank's responses and suggesting more empathetic approaches.

2. Virtual Reality (VR) Social Skill Training:

- A VR program provided Mayank with immersive experiences that mimicked challenging social interactions in professional settings. The AI-driven system adjusted scenarios based on Mayank's performance, gradually increasing complexity and helping him practice patience, active listening, and constructive feedback.

3. AI-Assisted Cognitive Behavioral Therapy (CBT):

- Alongside traditional therapy sessions, Mayank used an AI chatbot that delivered CBT techniques to address and modify his thought patterns. The chatbot helped identify instances of narcissistic thinking and provided strategies to develop a more balanced self-image and healthier interpersonal dynamics.

4. Wearable Technology for Emotional Regulation:

- Mayank also used a wearable device that monitored physiological indicators of stress and provided alerts to practice emotional regulation techniques. This instant feedback helped him manage stress in real-time, reducing instances of reactive behavior.

Outcome:

After six months of consistent use of these AI-assisted interventions, Mayank experienced significant improvements:

- Enhanced Empathy: Mayank reported a newfound ability to understand colleagues' perspectives, leading to more cooperative and less confrontational interactions at work.

- Improved Emotional Regulation: The wearable device helped Mayank recognize and manage stress before it escalated into conflicts, making him more resilient in facing workplace challenges.

- Better Feedback Reception: Through VR and the behavioral therapy app, Mayank learned to accept and constructively use feedback, seeing it as an opportunity for growth rather than criticism.

- Sustained Employment: For the first time in several years, Mayank was able to maintain his job for over a year, receiving positive evaluations from his supervisors and peers.

Conclusion:

Mayank's case demonstrates the potential of AI-assisted interventions in supporting individuals with narcissistic personality patterns to overcome interpersonal challenges in the workplace. By integrating technology with traditional therapy, Mayank was able to develop the skills necessary for job stability, highlighting the transformative power of AI in addressing complex psychological patterns.

AI and Subconscious Energy Healing for Narcissistic Personality Patterns

Subconscious energy healing therapy augmented by AI offers a promising approach to managing narcissistic personality patterns by targeting underlying psychological and emotional factors. Here's an overview of how AI can enhance subconscious energy healing therapy in this context:

1. Personalized Treatment Plans:

AI algorithms can analyze vast amounts of data, including individual's psychological profiles, behavioral patterns, and treatment responses, to generate personalized treatment plans tailored to each person's unique needs and characteristics.

2. Real-time Feedback and Monitoring:

AI-powered tools can provide real-time feedback during therapy sessions, alerting both the therapist and the individual to subtle shifts in emotional states or energy imbalances. This allows for immediate adjustments to the treatment approach and enhances the effectiveness of the therapy.

3. Pattern Recognition and Analysis:

AI algorithms can identify patterns in thought processes, emotional responses, and behavior associated with narcissistic personality patterns. By recognizing these patterns, therapists can target specific areas for intervention and track progress over time.

4. Virtual Reality (VR) Integration:

VR technology, enhanced by AI, can create immersive environments that facilitate subconscious exploration and healing. Individuals can engage in guided visualization exercises or virtual scenarios designed to promote self-reflection, empathy development, and emotional regulation.

5. Natural Language Processing (NLP) for Reflection and Insight:

NLP algorithms can analyze written or spoken reflections from therapy sessions, identifying key themes, emotions, and cognitive distortions associated with narcissistic tendencies. This information can then be used to guide further exploration and promote insight and self-awareness.

6. Biofeedback Integration:

AI-powered biofeedback devices can monitor physiological indicators of stress, such as heart rate variability and skin conductance, during therapy sessions. This data can inform therapists about the individual's stress levels and guide relaxation techniques or interventions to regulate emotional arousal.

7. Predictive Modeling for Long-term Outcomes:

By analyzing historical treatment data and individual characteristics, AI algorithms can generate predictive models to forecast long-term treatment outcomes. This information can help therapists and individuals set realistic goals, track progress, and make informed decisions about ongoing care.

8. Continuous Learning and Adaptation:

AI systems can continuously learn from new data and treatment experiences, refining their algorithms and recommendations over time. This adaptive approach ensures that therapy remains dynamic and responsive to the evolving needs and preferences of individuals with narcissistic personality patterns.

Conclusion:

By integrating AI technologies into subconscious energy healing therapy, therapists can enhance the effectiveness and efficiency of treatment for individuals with narcissistic personality patterns. These AI-driven approaches offer personalized, data-driven interventions that target underlying psychological mechanisms, promote self-awareness and insight, and support long-term emotional healing and growth.

Case Study: Deepak's Journey to Self-Discovery and Healing

Background:

Deepak, a 35-year-old entrepreneur from Mumbai, had been struggling with interpersonal relationships and maintaining successful business partnerships. He exhibited traits consistent with narcissistic personality patterns, including a constant need for admiration, difficulty empathizing with others, and a tendency to manipulate situations to his advantage.

Intervention:

Deepak sought help from a holistic therapist who specialized in subconscious energy healing therapy, augmented by AI technologies. The therapist, Dr. Patel, designed a personalized treatment plan for Deepak, integrating AI-driven tools to enhance the therapeutic process.

1. **Personalized Treatment Plan:**

- Dr. Patel utilized AI algorithms to analyze Deepak's psychological profile, identifying specific cognitive and emotional patterns associated with narcissistic tendencies. Based on this analysis, Dr. Patel tailored a treatment plan focused on promoting self-awareness, empathy development, and emotional regulation.

2. **Real-time Feedback and Monitoring:**

- During therapy sessions, Deepak wore a biofeedback device equipped with AI capabilities to monitor his physiological responses, such as heart rate variability and skin conductance. The AI system provided real-time feedback to Deepak and Dr.

Patel, alerting them to changes in emotional arousal and guiding relaxation techniques as needed.

3. **Virtual Reality (VR) Integration**:

- Deepak engaged in VR-based guided visualization exercises, facilitated by AI-driven virtual environments. These immersive experiences allowed Deepak to explore subconscious thoughts and emotions related to his narcissistic patterns, promoting self-reflection and insight.

4. **Natural Language Processing (NLP) Analysis**:

- Deepak journalized his thoughts and reflections after each therapy session, which were then analyzed using NLP algorithms. The AI system identified recurring themes and cognitive distortions in Deepak's reflections, helping Dr. Patel guide further exploration and cognitive restructuring.

5. **Predictive Modeling for Long-term Outcomes**:

- AI algorithms analyzed historical treatment data and individual characteristics to generate predictive models of Deepak's long-term treatment outcomes. This information informed Dr. Patel and Deepak about realistic expectations and milestones for the therapy journey.

Outcome:

Over the course of twelve months, Deepak experienced significant improvements:

- **Increased Self-awareness**: Deepak gained insight into his narcissistic tendencies and their impact on his relationships and business interactions.

- **Enhanced Empathy**: Through VR experiences and empathetic listening exercises, Deepak developed a greater capacity to understand and empathize with others' perspectives.

- Improved Emotional Regulation: Utilizing biofeedback and relaxation techniques, Deepak learned to manage stress and emotional arousal more effectively, reducing impulsive and reactive behaviors.

- **Strengthened Relationships**: Deepak's newfound self-awareness and empathy led to healthier and more authentic connections with family members, friends, and business associates.

Conclusion:

Deepak's journey exemplifies the transformative potential of AI-enhanced subconscious energy healing therapy in managing narcissistic personality patterns. By leveraging AI technologies to augment traditional therapeutic approaches, individuals like Deepak can embark on a path of self-discovery, healing, and personal growth, ultimately leading to more fulfilling and harmonious lives.

Optimism and hope for victims of abuse from Narsisistic Individuals

Yes, there is hope for people going through narcissistic abuse. While navigating narcissistic relationships can be incredibly challenging, recovery and healing are possible with the right support and resources. Here are some reasons for hope:

1. **Awareness and Understanding**: Recognizing narcissistic abuse is the first step toward healing. By understanding the dynamics of narcissistic behavior and its impact on their lives, individuals can begin to reclaim their power and make informed decisions about their well-being.

2. **Seeking Support**: There are many resources available for individuals experiencing narcissistic abuse, including therapy, support groups, hotlines, and online communities. Seeking support from professionals and others who have experienced similar situations can provide validation, guidance, and encouragement.

3. **Setting Boundaries:** Learning to set and enforce boundaries is crucial for protecting oneself from further harm in narcissistic relationships. With support and guidance, individuals can develop healthier boundaries and assert themselves in relationships, reducing the impact of narcissistic abuse.

4. **Healing Trauma**: Narcissistic abuse can cause significant emotional and psychological trauma. However, with the help of therapy and other healing modalities, individuals can

address and process their trauma, leading to greater resilience and well-being.

5. **Building Self-Esteem**: Narcissistic abuse often erodes self-esteem and self-worth. Through therapy, self-care practices, and supportive relationships, individuals can rebuild their self-esteem and develop a more positive sense of self.

6. **Creating a Supportive Network:** Surrounding oneself with supportive friends, family members, and professionals who understand and validate their experiences can provide invaluable support and encouragement on the journey to healing.

While healing from narcissistic abuse may take time and effort, it is possible to break free from the cycle of abuse and build a happier, healthier life. With perseverance, self-compassion, and support, individuals can overcome the effects of narcissistic abuse and thrive.

In Conclusion: Empowerment Through Understanding and Collaboration

In "Navigating Narcissism: Collaborative Team Approach and Family Therapy for Empowerment," we have journeyed through the complex landscape of narcissistic behaviors, their impact on individuals and families, and the transformative power of a collaborative therapeutic approach. The book underscores the critical need for a nuanced understanding of narcissism, not as a label to be used pejoratively but as a spectrum of behaviors that can profoundly affect relationships and family dynamics.

The collaborative team approach, emphasizing the integration of individual therapy, family therapy, and broader support systems, offers a roadmap for healing and empowerment. This methodology recognizes that the path to recovery is not solitary; it requires the concerted effort of professionals, the affected individuals, and their families. Through this collaboration, the book illustrates how the veil of confusion and pain that narcissistic behaviors often weave can be lifted, offering clarity and a path forward.

Family therapy, as detailed in this book, is not about assigning blame but about understanding the dynamics that contribute to unhealthy patterns. It serves as a powerful tool for change, providing all family members with the strategies and communication skills needed to rebuild trust, establish boundaries, and foster healthier relationships. This approach recognizes that each family member plays a role in the family system and has the potential to contribute to its healing and growth.

Empowerment, a central theme of this book, is achieved through knowledge, understanding, and the application of therapeutic strategies. It is about moving from a place of vulnerability and confusion to a position of strength and clarity. This empowerment enables individuals and families to not only navigate the challenges posed by narcissistic behaviors but also to emerge more resilient and connected.

As we conclude, it's important to acknowledge that the journey of healing from the effects of narcissism is ongoing. There will be challenges and setbacks, but with the right support and resources, growth and healing are possible. "Navigating Narcissism" aims to be a beacon of hope and a guide for those who find themselves struggling within these dynamics. It encourages a shift from despair to action, from isolation to community, and from hurt to healing.

In closing, let us remember that the journey toward healing and empowerment is a testament to the human spirit's resilience. By adopting a collaborative team approach and embracing the principles of family therapy, there is hope for a future where relationships are defined not by manipulation and pain, but by mutual respect, understanding, and love.

Glossary

A

- AI (Artificial Intelligence): A branch of computer science dedicated to creating systems capable of performing tasks that typically require human intelligence, such as learning, decision-making, and speech recognition.

- Algorithm: A set of rules or instructions given to an AI system to help it learn from data and make decisions or predictions based on it.

B

- Behavioral Therapy: A type of psychotherapy that focuses on changing negative or destructive behaviors through conditioning and reinforcement strategies.

C

- Cognitive Behavioral Therapy (CBT): A psychotherapeutic treatment that helps individuals understand the thoughts and feelings that influence behaviors. CBT is commonly used to treat a wide range of disorders, including depression, anxiety, and phobias.

D

- Data Analysis: The process of inspecting, cleansing, transforming, and modeling data with the goal of discovering useful information, informing conclusions, and supporting decision-making.

E

- Emotional Intelligence: The ability to recognize, understand, and manage our own emotions and to recognize, understand, and influence the emotions of others.

F

- Feedback Loop: A system used to gather and use information to regulate and guide an AI system or human behavior towards a desired goal.

G

- Generalization: In machine learning, the ability of a model to perform well on new, unseen data after having been trained on a training dataset.

H

- Heuristic: A problem-solving approach that uses a practical method or various shortcuts to produce solutions that may not be optimal but are sufficient for the immediate goals.

I

- Interpersonal Skills: The skills used by a person to interact with others effectively. In the workplace, interpersonal skills are considered a type of soft skills.

J

- Job Stability: The likelihood of an individual to maintain a particular job for a long period without facing termination or significant problems.

K

- Knowledge Base: A centralized repository for information: a public library, a database of related information about a particular subject.

L

- Learning Algorithms: Algorithms that allow software applications to become more accurate in predicting outcomes without being explicitly programmed to do so.

M

- Machine Learning: A subset of AI that includes algorithms that enable computers to learn from and make decisions based on data.

N

- Narcissistic Personality Disorder (NPD): A mental condition characterized by a long-term pattern of exaggerated self-importance, the need for excessive attention and admiration, troubled relationships, and a lack of empathy for others.

O

- Open Communication: A form of communication where all parties freely exchange ideas and feelings, including those of criticism or disagreement.

P

- Psychoeducation: The process of providing education and information to those seeking or receiving mental health services, such as diagnoses, treatment options, and coping strategies.

Q

- Quantitative Data: Data that can be quantified and verified, and is amenable to statistical manipulation. Quantitative data defines whereas qualitative data describes.

R

- Reinforcement Learning: A type of machine learning algorithm that is based on the idea of rewarding desired behaviors and/or punishing undesired ones.

S

- Stress Management: Techniques and psychotherapies aimed at controlling a person's levels of stress, especially chronic stress, usually for the purpose of improving everyday functioning.

T

- Therapeutic Intervention: An action or set of actions taken by health professionals to help someone with a physical, mental, or emotional issue.

U

- User Interface (UI): The means by which the user and a computer system interact, in particular the use of input devices and software.

V

- Virtual Reality (VR): A simulated experience that can be similar to or completely different from the real world. It is used in various applications, from entertainment to medical training.

W

- Wearable Technology: Electronic devices that are worn on the body as accessories or part of clothing, capable of collecting data and often offering specific functionalities, such as fitness tracking.

X

- XML (Extensible Mayankup Language): A flexible text format used for the structured storage and transport of data, used in a wide variety of data interchange applications.

Y

- Yield: In the context of performance metrics, the amount of useful or desired output from a system, process, or product.

Z

- Zero-Sum Game: A situation in social science and economic theory where one participant's gains result directly from another's losses.

www.ingramcontent.com/pod-product-compliance
Lightning Source LLC
LaVergne TN
LVHW061541070526
838199LV00077B/6865